"Doubt kills more dreams than failure ever will."

– Suzy Kassem

Author's Message

Before you continue, I just wanted to say thank you for reading my book.

You could have picked from dozens of other cookbooks but you chose mine.

So, a HUGE thanks to you for getting this book and for taking the time to read it.

Now I wanted to ask you for a small favor. Could you please consider posting a review on the platform you purchased the book?

Getting reviews is one of the easiest ways to support my work and help me reach more people.

When you share something of value, people associate that value with you.

If the book helps them, people will feel grateful to you because you are the one that has shared it with them. So it's a win-win situation.

Your feedback is important to me and will help more people benefit from the book.

So if you enjoyed it, please leave an honest review. (It only takes a few seconds)

Thanks, Kathy

P.S. It means a lot to me to hear your opinion back.

Table of Contents

Meals

Roast chicken

Turkey with rice

Spicy ground beef

Chicken stir fry

Eggs with spinach

Rice with spinach

Spinach Pancakes

Broccoli meatballs

Stuffed peppers

Stuffed tomatoes

Salmon w/ veggies

Quinoa peppers

Meals

34
Chicken w/ mango

35
Zucchini noodles

36
Turkey meatballs

37
Simple spaghetti

38
Mushroom spaghetti

39
Mediterranean spaghetti

40
Shrimp spaghetti

41
Oatmeal w/ banana

Salads

Spinach salad

Salmon salad

Carrot salad

Chicken Salad

Shopska salad

Cod fish salad

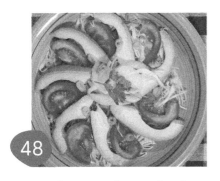
Avocado salad

Cabbage salad

Broccoli salad

Quinoa salad

Tomato salad

Cucumber Salad

Salads

Forest fruit salad

Greek salad

Mediterranean salad

Caprese Salad

Quinoa & tomato

Strawberry salad

Mexican mix salad

Tomato & spinach

Soups

62
Bean soup

63
Fish soup

64
Chicken soup

65
Mushroom soup

66
Zucchini soup

67
Pea soup

68
Tomato soup

69
Spinach cream soup

70
Red lentil soup

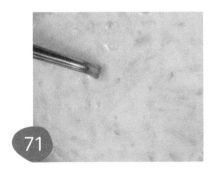
71
Tarator

72
Veal broccoli soup

73
Creamy avocado soup

Soups

74 Broccoli & spinach

75 Asparagus soup

76 Vegetable soup

77 Broccoli soup

78 Creamy mushroom

79 Potato cream soup

80 Minestrone soup

81 Mexican lentils soup

Desserts

82

Banana cupcake

83

Berry ice cream

84

Chia pudding

85

Apple omelette

86

Apple pie

87

Baked pears

88

Carrot cake outmeal

89

Banana coconut cake

90

Avocado cheesecake

91

Greek yogurt
cheesecake

Smoothies

Apple Smoothie
92

Pumpkin Smoothie
93

Coffee Smoothie
94

Banana Smoothie
95

Avocado Smoothie
96

Mango Smoothie
97

Tropical fruit Smoothie
98

Green Smoothie
99

Pineapple Smoothie
100

Pineapple & mango
101

Strawberry & banana
102

Orange Smoothie
103

Smoothies

104

Apple & spinach

105

Banana & berry

106

Tropical green

Burgers

Chicken & avocado

Portobello mushroom

Grilled chicken

Veggie burger

BBQ Pork burger

Mediterranean pork

The simple burger

Tilapia burger

Salmon & zucchini

Grilled salmon burger

Pizzas

117

Whole wheat veggie

118

Pesto & spinach

119

Mushroom veggie pizza

120

Avocado & pesto

121

Tuna & mushrooms

Part 2: The basics

What is the Mediterranean diet?

The Mediterranean diet is a dietary pattern that is based on the traditional eating habits of countries surrounding the Mediterranean Sea, such as Greece, Italy, Spain, and Morocco.

The diet is characterized by high consumption of plant-based foods, such as fruits, vegetables, whole grains, legumes, nuts, and seeds, along with olive oil as the primary source of fat.

Fish and seafood are also an essential part of the diet, while dairy products, poultry, and red meat are consumed in moderation. The Mediterranean diet is also known for its moderate consumption of red wine during meals.

Numerous studies have linked the Mediterranean diet to a reduced risk of chronic diseases, such as heart disease, stroke, and type 2 diabetes, as well as improved cognitive function and longevity.

The Mediterranean diet has been linked to numerous health benefits. Here are some of them:

1. **Reduced risk of heart disease**: The Mediterranean diet has been associated with a lower risk of heart disease and stroke. This is believed to be due to its emphasis on plant-based foods, healthy fats (such as olive oil), and lean proteins like fish.

1. **Improved brain function**: Some research suggests that the Mediterranean diet may help protect against age-related cognitive decline and reduce the risk of dementia.

2. **Lower risk of certain cancers**: Studies have found that the Mediterranean diet may be associated with a lower risk of certain cancers, such as breast cancer and colon cancer.

The benefits of the Mediterranean diet

The Mediterranean diet has been linked to numerous health benefits. Here are some of them:

1. **Reduced risk of heart disease**: The Mediterranean diet has been associated with a lower risk of heart disease and stroke. This is believed to be due to its emphasis on plant-based foods, healthy fats (such as olive oil), and lean proteins like fish.

2. **Improved brain function**: Some research suggests that the Mediterranean diet may help protect against age-related cognitive decline and reduce the risk of dementia.

3. **Lower risk of certain cancers**: Studies have found that the Mediterranean diet may be associated with a lower risk of certain cancers, such as breast cancer and colon cancer.

4. **Weight loss and management**: The Mediterranean diet emphasizes whole, nutrient-dense foods that are filling and satisfying, which may make it easier to maintain a healthy weight.

5. **Improved gut health**: The Mediterranean diet is rich in fiber from fruits, vegetables, and whole grains, which can promote healthy digestion and a healthy gut microbiome.

6. **Reduced inflammation**: The diet's emphasis on anti-inflammatory foods, such as fruits, vegetables, and healthy fats, may help reduce chronic inflammation in the body.

7. **Longevity**: Some studies have suggested that following a Mediterranean-style diet may be associated with a longer lifespan.

Overall, the Mediterranean diet is a balanced and sustainable way of eating that emphasizes whole, nutrient-dense foods and has been linked to a range of health benefits.

What to eat

The Mediterranean diet emphasizes whole, nutrient-dense foods, and encourages a variety of plant-based foods, healthy fats, and lean proteins. Here are some examples of foods to eat on the Mediterranean diet:

1. **Vegetables**: All types of vegetables, including leafy greens, tomatoes, peppers, onions, and eggplant.
2. **Fruits**: All types of fruit, including berries, citrus, melons, and figs.
3. **Whole grains**: Such as brown rice, whole-wheat pasta, and quinoa.
4. **Legumes**: Including beans, lentils, and chickpeas.
5. **Nuts and seeds**: Such as almonds, walnuts, sunflower seeds, and chia seeds.
6. **Healthy fats**: Including olive oil, avocado, nuts, and seeds.
7. **Fish and seafood**: Such as salmon, tuna, shrimp, and mussels.

8. **Poultry**: Such as chicken and turkey.
9. **Dairy**: Including yogurt, cheese, milk in moderation.
10. **Red wine**: In moderation.

It's important to note that the Mediterranean diet is not about strict rules or limitations, but rather about incorporating a variety of whole, nutrient-dense foods in your meals.

What to avoid

The Mediterranean diet is not a restrictive diet, but there are some foods and ingredients that are limited or avoided in this dietary pattern. Here are some examples:

1. **Processed foods**: Foods that are highly processed, including sugary drinks, refined grains, and packaged snacks, are generally avoided on the Mediterranean diet.
2. **Red meat**: While lean proteins like poultry and fish are encouraged on the Mediterranean diet, red meat is generally limited but if you like it there isn't any problem with consuming it from time to time.
3. **Sweets and desserts**: Processed sweets and desserts are generally not recommended on the Mediterranean diet, but small amounts of natural sweeteners like honey or maple syrup can be used in moderation. It is not a problem if you eat homemade sweets and desserts from time to time in moderation. As long as you know exactly what's inside and how many calories you consume it's not a bad idea to reward yourself for your good eating habits and hard work.
4. **Butter and other unhealthy fats**: Instead, the Mediterranean diet emphasizes healthy fats like olive oil, avocado, nuts, and seeds.

5. **Salt**: While salt is not entirely avoided on the Mediterranean diet, it is limited, and herbs and spices are used to add flavor to dishes. Of course, most meals will not taste very good without any salt so use it in moderation when you have to.

Overall, the Mediterranean diet emphasizes whole, nutrient-dense foods and minimizes highly processed foods, added sugars, and unhealthy fats. That's why it's perfect for healthy eating and weight loss or muscle development.

How to lose weight 101

Losing weight is a simple process. If you want to lose weight you need to create a consistent calorie deficit, which means consuming fewer calories than your body needs daily to maintain its current weight.

Example: If your body needs 1200 calories daily you can lose weight healthily by consuming only 1100. (Please note: the number of calories per person varies and must be calculated accordingly)

Here are some steps to follow if you want to lose weight:

Step 1: Calculate your daily calorie needs

Use an online calculator or consult with a dietitian to determine your daily calorie needs based on factors such as your age, sex, weight, height, and activity level.

Here is the Harris-Benedict equation for calculating your daily calorie needs:

1. Calculate your Basal Metabolic Rate (BMR)

For lbs and inches: BMR = 655 + (4.35 x weight in lbs) + (4.7 x height in inches) - (4.7 x age in years)

For kg and cm: BMR = 88.4 + (13.4 x weight in kg) + (4.8 x height in cm) - (5.68 x age in years)

2. Determine your Total Daily Energy Expenditure (TDEE)

TDEE = BMR x activity factor

Activity factors:
1. Sedentary: 1.2
2. Lightly Active: 1.375
3. Moderately Active: 1.55
4. Very Active: 1.725
5. Extremely Active: 1.9

3. Create a calorie deficit

To lose weight, consume fewer calories than your TDEE. A safe deficit is 200-500 fewer calories per day.

4. Monitor your progress

Track once a week your weight and body measurements (arms, legs, waist, hip, etc) using a measuring tape to monitor your progress and make adjustments to your diet and exercise routine as needed.

Example: If you don't lose any weight and the body measurements don't change, lower your calorie intake by 100-200 calories for the next week.

It's important to remember that these calculations are just estimates, and individual calorie needs may vary depending on many factors. Consult with a healthcare professional or registered dietitian for personalized guidance and support.

Should you exercise for weight loss?

Yes, working out can be an **effective way to support weight loss** based on scientific evidence.

Exercise can help create a calorie deficit **by burning calories**, and it can also help preserve lean body mass while losing weight, which is important for maintaining metabolic rate and overall health.

In addition to the calorie-burning benefits, regular exercise can also **improve insulin sensitivity, reduce inflammation, and increase muscle strength and endurance**, all of which can support weight loss efforts.

The American College of Sports Medicine recommends at least **150 minutes of moderate-intensity exercise per week**, or 75 minutes of vigorous-intensity exercise per week, for general health benefits.

To support weight loss, more exercise may be necessary, and it's important to also **include resistance training to build and maintain muscle mass**.

However, it's important to note that exercise alone may not be sufficient for significant weight loss, especially **if dietary habits are not also addressed**. A combination of regular exercise and a healthy diet that creates a calorie deficit is generally recommended for sustainable weight loss.

How to use the Mediterranean diet to lose weight

The Mediterranean diet can be a helpful tool for weight loss because it emphasizes whole, nutrient-dense foods that are lower in calories and higher in fiber, protein, and healthy fats.

It is also proven that foods rich in fiber, proteins, and healthy fats do make you feel fuller for longer periods of time which will result in eating less food during the day. Another plus is that by eating a high volume of healthy, nutrient-dense foods you feel full and satisfied without consuming too many calories.

Here are some tips for using the Mediterranean diet to lose weight:

1. **Focus on whole, unprocessed foods**: Choose whole grains, fruits, vegetables, legumes, nuts, seeds, and lean proteins like fish and poultry. These foods are typically lower in calories and higher in nutrients than processed foods.
2. **Use healthy fats**: The Mediterranean diet includes healthy fats like olive oil, nuts, and avocados. These foods can help you feel full and satisfied while providing important nutrients.
3. **Limit high-calorie foods**: While the Mediterranean diet is not strictly a low-calorie diet, it's important to limit high-calorie foods.
4. **Practice portion control**: Even healthy foods can contribute to weight gain if consumed in large amounts. Pay attention to portion sizes and eat mindfully to avoid overeating.
5. **Be physically active**: The Mediterranean lifestyle also emphasizes regular physical activity. Aim for at least 30 minutes of moderate-intensity exercise most days of the week to support weight loss.

Remember, weight loss is about creating a calorie deficit, so it's important to adjust portion sizes and total calorie intake to align with your weight loss goals.

FAQ about the Mediterranean diet

Q: **Is the Mediterranean diet suitable for vegetarians or vegans?**
A: Yes, the Mediterranean diet can be adapted to suit a vegetarian or vegan lifestyle by focusing on plant-based sources of protein like legumes, tofu, and tempeh.

Q: **Is it necessary to count calories on the Mediterranean diet?**
A: The Mediterranean diet is not strictly a low-calorie diet, but weight loss still requires creating a calorie deficit. While calorie counting is not necessary, it's important to be mindful of portion sizes and total calorie intake to align with weight loss goals.

Q: **Can I still enjoy wine on the Mediterranean diet?**
A: Yes, moderate consumption of wine is a part of the Mediterranean lifestyle, but it's important to limit intake to one or two glasses per day and choose red wine for its potential health benefits. But of course, drinking wine is optional.

Q: **Is the Mediterranean diet suitable for people with food allergies or intolerances?**
A: The Mediterranean diet is relatively flexible and can be adapted to accommodate food allergies or intolerances. Consult with a healthcare professional or registered dietitian for personalized guidance.

Q: **Can I eat dairy on the Mediterranean diet?**
A: Yes, dairy can be included in the Mediterranean diet in moderation. Choose low-fat or non-fat dairy products like Greek yogurt and cheese.

Q: **Is it necessary to cook with olive oil on the Mediterranean diet?**
A: While cooking with olive oil is a hallmark of the Mediterranean diet, other healthy fats like avocado oil and canola oil can also be used.

Q: **Do I need to eat fish on the Mediterranean diet?**
A: While fish is a common component of the Mediterranean diet, it is not a requirement. Vegetarian and vegan sources of protein like legumes, tofu, and tempeh can be included instead.

Q: **Is the Mediterranean diet appropriate for people with high blood pressure?**
A: The Mediterranean diet may be beneficial for people with high blood pressure, as it emphasizes whole, nutrient-dense foods that can support heart health. However, it's important to consult with a healthcare professional or registered dietitian for personalized guidance.

Part 3: The 30-day meal plan

The 30-day meal plan

We know that restricting yourself too much will lead to failure. That's why we will give you only a basic outline of the type of meals to eat. It's entirely up to you to choose the meal or the type.

And remember that you can change the order or add/remove meals depending on your lifestyle and goals.

How it works: Just replace each type of meal with one of the recipes included in this book. Pick any one of the given categories and choose any recipe you like. Repeat for 30 days the same structure and only change the recipes and type of meals to your liking.

Example: For breakfast, I will go with a smoothie which is going to be the "Banana smoothie"

Daily Plan

- **Meal 1**: Breakfast (Smoothie, Salad)
- **Meal 2**: Lunch (Meal, Soup, Salad, Burger, Pizza)
- **Meal 3**: Snack (Fruits, Veggies, Something healthy and light)
- **Meal 4**: Dinner (Meal, Soup, Salad, Burger, Pizza)

Rewards: If you are on the right track and are eating healthy, doing some type of physical activity and improving your health you can replace the snack with a dessert recipe once a week to reward yourself.

Tracking Calories: Every recipe in this book has calories and nutrients per portion and about the whole meal. Use that info to track down calories and make sure you are in a caloric deficit. Use a physical book or online app to write down your calories like Myfitnesspal (it's free).

Just be careful not to get too obsessed about calories because it may have negative long-term results. Do it mainly in the beginning as you are building the right daily habits. In time you will get used to the food and will be able to make better food decisions.

After 30 days

Long term weight loss results take way longer than 30 days. If after 30 days of following the Mediterranean diet, you are on the right track and seeing results just continue doing the exact same thing as before and adapt the portion sizes and meals according to your progress.

Your main goal is to build the right habits that will help you lose weight and keep it off.

Roast Chicken Breast

3 servings

Prep: 5 min | Cook: 25 min | Total: 30 min

Ingredients

- ○ 1.4 lbs of chicken breast (700g)
- ○ 2 tbsp olive oil (26g)
- ○ 1 tbsp paprika
- ○ Salt (by taste)
- ○ 1 cup of water
- ○ Black pepper (optional)
- ○ 1 pinch chopped parsley (optional)
- ○ 2 cloves of garlic (optional)
- ○ 1 tbsp lemon juice (optional)

Method

1. Turn on the oven or air fryer and preheat it to 480F (250C) for a couple of minutes.

2. Meanwhile, wash well and place the chicken breasts into a large enough non-stick tray. (You can also add some baking paper for easier cleaning)

3. Pour on top the meat olive oil, paprika, and salt.

4. Mix well so all pieces of meat are well covered with the ingredients on all sides. You can optionally add chopped garlic or black pepper for extra flavor.

5. Pour 1 cup of water into the tray.

6. Roast the chicken breast for about 30 minutes until they become slightly brown. Use a fork to check them and flip them over after 15 minutes so the meat is cooked evenly on both sides.

7. Serve the ready meal with a pinch of chopped parsley and a bit of lemon juice.

8. Split into 3 equal portions and meal prep for 3 days (optional)

Nutrition: 1 serving / whole meal, calories 373 / 1120, protein(g) 47 / 142, carbs(g) 1 / 4, fats(g) 18 / 56, fiber(g) 0 / 1, sodium(mg) 146 / 440, sugar(g) 0 / 0, saturated fat(g) 3 / 10

Baked Turkey with Rice
5 servings

Prep: 10 min | Cook: 2 h 50 min | Total: 3 h 0 min

Ingredients

- ○ 1 cup of raw brown rice (200 g)
- ○ 2 medium turkey legs/wings (651 g)
- ○ 1 medium head of onion (160 g)
- ○ 3 cloves of garlic
- ○ 1 large tomato or 2 small ones (200 g)
- ○ 1 medium carrot (60 g)
- ○ 1 tbsp olive oil
- ○ 1 and 1/2 cups of chicken broth 1:1.5 ratio (cubes or liquid) (350 ml)
- ○ 1 tbsp paprika
- ○ 1 tbsp onion powder
- ○ 1 tbsp garlic powder
- ○ 1 tbsp parsley flakes
- ○ 1 tbsp salt (by taste)
- ○ 1 tbsp black pepper (by taste)

Method

1. Wash, peel, and cut the garlic, onion, tomatoes, and carrots into small pieces.
2. Spread olive oil into a big non-stick tray and place the meat inside.
3. Cover evenly with olive oil, onion powder, garlic powder, paprika, black pepper, and salt. Use your hands to mix all the spices nicely on all sides.
4. Take the meat out of the tray, evenly add the washed rice, and pour the chicken broth.
5. Lay down carefully the pieces of meat over the rice, while leaving only half of the meat in the broth. Add all the chopped vegetables evenly on top and sprinkle the parsley flakes.
6. Cover the tray with aluminum foil and bake for 2 hours in a preheated oven at 350F (180C). (it may be less if you use a convection oven)
7. After 2 hours (or less) remove the foil and bake for 50 minutes more without anything.
8. Once done, wait for 10-15 mins to cool down and split into equal portions.

Nutrition: 1 serving / whole meal, calories 427 / 2135, protein(g) 33 / 166, carbs(g) 32 / 163, fats(g) 18 / 92, fiber(g) 3 / 17, sodium(mg) 996 / 4980, sugar(g) 2 / 12, saturated fat(g) 4 / 21

Spicy Ground Beef
4 servings

Prep: 5 min | Cook: 20 min | Total: 25 min

Ingredients

- ○ 1 pound ground beef chuck (500 g)
- ○ 0.5 lbs cherry tomatoes, chopped (250 g)
- ○ 4 tsp chili powder
- ○ 1 tsp ground cumin
- ○ 1 tsp paprika
- ○ 1 tsp sugar
- ○ ½ tsp onion powder
- ○ ¼ tsp crushed red pepper
- ○ 1 tbsp olive oil
- ○ 3 cloves garlic, chopped
- ○ Salt and black pepper by taste
- ○ Salad by choice(optional)

Method

1. Combine all the spices in a small bowl and mix well. Set aside.

2. Heat the olive oil in a large skillet over medium-high heat. Add the garlic and cook until fragrant (about 30 seconds)

3. Add the ground beef and chili mixture and cook, breaking up the beef with a spoon, until brown.

4. Add the chopped tomatoes, and the spices mix and cook, stirring, until heated through.

5. Separate in equal portions and eat with salad by choice. You can even make healthy tacos with the meat.

Nutrition: 1 serving / whole meal, calories 380 / 1520, protein(g) 24 / 98, carbs(g) 5 / 21, fats(g) 29 / 116, fiber(g) 1 / 6, sodium(mg) 220 / 880, sugar(g) 3 / 12, saturated fat(g) 11 / 46

Chicken Stir Fry

4 servings

Prep: 5 min | Cook: 20 min | Total: 25 min

Ingredients

- ○ 1 lb boneless, skinless chicken breast, sliced into thin strips (500g)
- ○ 2 medium carrots, julienned
- ○ 1 cup frozen peas
- ○ 1 red bell pepper, sliced
- ○ 1 yellow bell pepper, sliced
- ○ 1 zucchini, sliced
- ○ 1 medium onion, sliced
- ○ 2 cloves garlic, minced
- ○ 2 tbsp vegetable oil
- ○ 1 tbsp soy sauce
- ○ Salt and pepper to taste

Method

1. Heat the oil in a large wok or skillet over high heat.
2. Add the chicken strips and stir-fry for 3-4 minutes or until lightly browned on all sides. Remove the chicken from the pan and set aside.
3. In the same pan, add the garlic and onion and stir-fry for 1-2 minutes or until the onion is translucent.
4. Add the carrots and stir-fry for 2-3 minutes or until slightly softened.
5. Add the bell peppers and zucchini and stir-fry for another 2-3 minutes or until the vegetables are slightly softened but still crunchy.
6. Add the frozen peas and stir-fry for 1-2 minutes or until the peas are heated through.
7. Add the cooked chicken back into the pan and stir to combine.
8. Drizzle soy sauce over the stir-fry and stir to coat the vegetables and chicken evenly.
9. Season with salt and pepper to taste.

Nutrition: 1 serving / whole meal, calories 257 / 1030, protein(g) 29 / 116, carbs(g) 7 / 29, fats(g) 12 / 50, fiber(g) 2 / 9, sodium(mg) 150 / 600, sugar(g) 3 / 12, saturated fat(g) 1 / 6

Eggs with Spinach

3 servings

Prep: 10 min | Cook: 40 min | Total: 50 min

Ingredients

- 8 medium whole eggs
- ¼ cup of milk (50g)
- 1/2 cup chopped leek (45 g)
- 1 tbsp chopped parsley
- 1 tbsp olive oil
- 1 ½ cups of chopped spinach (45 g)
- 2 oz of cow's white cheese (50 g)
- 1 large tomato or 2 small ones (200 g)
- Salt and black pepper by taste

Method

1. Wash and chop into small pieces the leek, parsley, tomatoes, and spinach. (keep the chopped spinach away from the rest)

2. In a big bowl, beat the eggs with the milk, and then add the chopped leek, parsley, spinach, salt, and black pepper and mix everything well.

3. In a deep preheated pan on high heat with olive oil, add the spinach and cook it for about 3 minutes while flipping it from time to time.

4. Pour the egg mixture into the spinach and stir. Once the eggs are nearly complete, break them into large pieces.

5. Turn off the heat and add the tomatoes and the cheese (make sure it fully melts). Mix well.

6. Split into equal portions and eat while still hot.

Nutrition: 1 serving / whole meal, calories 270 / 810, protein(g) 17 / 51, carbs(g) 5 / 16, fats(g) 20 / 60, fiber(g) 1 / 4, sodium(mg) 400 / 1200, sugar(g) 2 / 8, saturated fat(g) 8 / 24

Rice with Spinach

3 servings

Prep: 10 min | Cook: 40 min | Total: 50 min

Ingredients

- ○ 1 cup of brown rice (200 g)
- ○ 1 medium head of onion (160 g)
- ○ 1 clove of garlic
- ○ 1 medium carrot (60 g)
- ○ 1 lb spinach (500 g)
- ○ 2 tbsp olive oil (26.6 g)
- ○ 6 cups and 1/2 of water (1.5 liters)
- ○ Salt and black pepper (by taste)
- ○ Spearmint by taste
- ○ Pinch of chopped parsley (optional)

Method

1. Wash the rice well in a strainer with cold water until the water is clear.

2. Pour the water into a big pot and add the salt. Set it on high heat and wait for the water to boil. Once the water starts boiling, add the rice and let it simmer for 20 minutes on low heat with the lid on. Once ready let it rest in a bowl.

3. Meanwhile, wash, peel, and slice the garlic, onion, carrot, and spinach into small pieces. (keep the spinach in a different container)

4. Steam everything except the spinach in a pan with a lid on with olive oil, 3 tbsp of water for 8-10 minutes until the carrots are soft on medium heat.

5. Add the spinach to the pan and steam for 5 more mins. Next, add all the spices and stir well.

6. Once both the rice and the vegetables are ready, pour everything into a large tray, add 4 cups of water, and bake in a preheated oven at 400F (200C) until most water is vaporized. Once ready, split into equal portions. Add a bit of parsley on top.

Nutrition: 1 serving / whole meal, calories 275 / 825, protein(g) 6 / 19, carbs(g) 43 / 129, fats(g) 9 / 27, fiber(g) 4 / 14, sodium(mg) 81 / 245, sugar(g) 2 / 7, saturated fat(g) 1 / 4

Spinach Pancakes
1 serving

Prep: 10 min | Cook: 15 min | Total: 25 min

Ingredients

- ○ 2 large eggs
- ○ 0.5 lb spinach (250 g)
- ○ 1 medium tomato
- ○ 1 medium cucumber
- ○ 1 tbsp olive oil
- ○ Salt by taste

Method

1. Wash the spinach well and remove all the handles.
2. Place it inside the blender together with the eggs and a pinch of salt.
3. Blend until the mixture thickens.
4. With the help of a ladle (or you can directly use the blender jug) pour enough liquid, so it covers the bottom of a preheated pan with a bit of olive oil on medium heat.
5. Once the first side is ready, flip over and wait for the other side.
6. Do as many pancakes as you can and eat them while they are still hot.
7. You can fill them with chopped tomato and cucumber or any other combination as stuffing. (only include healthy stuff)

Nutrition: 1 serving / whole meal, calories 225 / 225, protein(g) 15 / 15, carbs(g) 9 / 9, fats(g) 16 / 16, fiber(g) 3 / 3, sodium(mg) 190 / 190, sugar(g) 5 / 5, saturated fat(g) 3 / 3

Broccoli Meatballs

1 serving

Prep: 10 min | Cook: 30 min | Total: 40 min

Ingredients

- ○ 1 lb/ large head of broccoli (500g)
- ○ 1 large egg
- ○ 1 tbsp olive oil
- ○ 4 sprigs of dill
- ○ Salt by taste

Method

1. Wash, break into smaller pieces, and steam the broccoli in a pan with a lid on with the olive oil, and 3 tbsp of water for 8-10 minutes until it is soft on medium heat. Remove all the water and leave to cool down.

2. Mash it down by hand with a masher in a large bowl or a machine until it becomes completely mashed.

3. Add the egg and the chopped small pieces of dill. Make sure to stir well.

4. When the mixture thickens enough, start forming meatballs of equal sizes.

5. Place them in a tray covered with baking paper and a bit of olive oil and bake in a preheated oven at 400F (200C). (make sure they are not touching one another)

6. Bake until they start getting a slight golden color.

Nutrition: 1 serving / whole meal, calories 200 / 200, protein(g) 11 / 11, carbs(g) 18 / 18, fats(g) 11 / 11, fiber(g) 9 / 9, sodium(mg) 190 / 190, sugar(g) 6 / 6, saturated fat(g) 2 / 2

Stuffed Peppers

5 servings

Prep: 10 min | Cook: 40 min | Total: 50 min

Ingredients

- ○ 8 medium red bell peppers
- ○ 1 lb ground beef (500g)
- ○ 4 medium carrots (240 g)
- ○ 4 medium tomatoes or 1 can dice tomatoes (14.5 oz) (400g)
- ○ 1 medium head of onion
- ○ 1 tbsp olive oil
- ○ 1 clove of garlic
- ○ Salt and black pepper by taste

Method

1. Wash, peel, and cut the carrots, onion, and garlic into very small pieces.

2. Steam them in a pan with a lid on with the olive oil, and 3 tbsp of water for 8-10 minutes until they are soft on medium heat. After 5 mins, add all the spices and stir well.

3. Add the can of tomatoes (or wash, clean, and mash regular tomatoes) to the mixture and stir. Add the ground beef while trying to split it into small pieces.

4. Cook and stir on medium heat for a few minutes while the mixture becomes thick.

5. Meanwhile, wash the peppers, cut the heads carefully, and remove the seeds. (your only hole should be in the head)

6. Once the mixture is thick, remove from heat and cool down a bit, fill all the peppers with it and place them in a tray covered with baking paper in a preheated oven at 350F (180C). Bake for 40 minutes.

7. Keep an eye every 10 minutes not to burn them. Remove when ready.

Nutrition: 1 serving / whole meal, calories 293 / 1468, protein(g) 16 / 81, carbs(g) 23 / 119, fats(g) 14 / 73, fiber(g) 7 / 35, sodium(mg) 265 / 1328, sugar(g) 9 / 47, saturated fat(g) 4 / 21

Stuffed Tomatoes

2 servings

Prep: 10 min | Cook: 30 min | Total: 40 min

Ingredients

- ○ 6 large tomatoes or 4 large tomatoes
- ○ 1 large egg
- ○ Salt by taste
- ○ 1 tsp olive oil
- ○ 2 pinches of black pepper (optional)

Method

1. Preheat an oven or an air fryer to 350F (180C).
2. Meanwhile, wash the tomatoes well with warm water and remove the stalks.
3. Cut clean the top part of the tomatoes and gently carve the inside out with a small spoon without damaging the walls or bottom. Collect the insides in a separate bowl or pour them directly into a blender. (If you don't have one you can use a handheld blender or a potato masher and a deep bowl)
4. Place the empty tomatoes into a large enough tray covered with baking paper. (You can spray it with a bit of oil as well)
5. Add the egg, olive oil, and salt into the blender and close the lid.
6. Blend for 30 sec to a minute until ready.
7. Gently pour the mixture into the tomatoes. Pour on top and around any leftover liquid.
8. Bake for about 30 minutes or until there is a slight crisp on top and all tomatoes are ready.
9. Split into 2 equal portions and eat within 1-3 days.

Nutrition: 1 serving / whole meal, calories 58 / 117, protein(g) 3 / 6, carbs(g) 7 / 14, fats(g) 2 / 5, fiber(g) 2 / 4, sodium(mg) 11 / 22, sugar(g) 4 / 9, saturated fat(g) 0 / 1

Grilled Salmon with Vegetables

4 servings

Prep: 10 min | Cook: 20 min | Total: 30 min

Ingredients

- ○ 4 salmon fillets (4oz each or 16oz total) (450g)
- ○ 4 cups of mixed vegetables (zucchini, red peppers, mushrooms, onions, etc.) (300g)
- ○ 1 tbsp olive oil (or oil spray)
- ○ 1 tsp dried oregano
- ○ Salt and pepper to taste

Method

1. Preheat the oven to 400°F. (200°C)
2. Toss vegetables with 1 tbsp olive oil and oregano in a large tray (you can add baking paper).
3. Season with salt and pepper. Spread evenly and roast for 20 minutes.
4. Meanwhile, season the salmon with salt and pepper and a bit of olive oil. Grill salmon for 3-4 minutes per side or until cooked through.
5. Once the veggies are ready serve the salmon with them.

Nutrition: 1 serving / whole meal, calories 165 / 663, protein(g) 17 / 70, carbs(g) 6 / 24, fats(g) 8 / 34, fiber(g) 2 / 10, sodium(mg) 38 / 153, sugar(g) 2 / 10, saturated fat(g) 1 / 5

Quinoa Stuffed Bell Peppers
4 servings

Prep: 15 min | Cook: 35 min | Total: 50 min

Ingredients

- ○ 4 normal bell peppers
- ○ 1 cup quinoa (185g)
- ○ 2 cups water
- ○ 1 can black beans, drained and rinsed (15 oz/400g)
- ○ 1 2/3 cups of sweet corn (250g) (frozen is preferred)
- ○ 1 medium onion, chopped
- ○ 1 tbsp olive oil
- ○ 1 tsp cumin
- ○ 1 tsp chili powder
- ○ Salt and pepper
- ○ 1/2 cup shredded feta cheese (60g)

Method

1. Preheat the oven to 375°F (190°C).
2. Cut the tops off the bell peppers and remove the seeds and membranes.
3. In a saucepan, bring quinoa and water to a boil. Cover and simmer for 15-20 minutes, until the water is absorbed.
4. In a skillet, heat the olive oil with, chili powder and onion until soft.
5. Add black beans, corn, cumin, salt, and pepper to the skillet and cook for a few minutes.
6. Add cooked quinoa to the skillet and mix well.
7. Stuff the bell peppers with the quinoa mixture and place them in a baking dish.
8. Bake for 20 minutes.
9. Sprinkle shredded feta cheese over the top of each pepper and bake for another 10-15 minutes, until the cheese is melted and bubbly.

Nutrition: 1 serving / whole meal, calories 339 / 1358, protein(g) 14 / 58, carbs(g) 53 / 215, fats(g) 10 / 40, fiber(g) 8 / 34, sodium(mg) 301 / 1204, sugar(g) 6 / 26, saturated fat(g) 4 / 16

Chicken with Mango Salsa
4 servings

Prep: 10 min | Cook: 15 min | Total: 25 min

Ingredients

- ○ 4 chicken breasts (1.2 lb / 540g)
- ○ Salt and pepper, to taste
- ○ 2 tbsp olive oil
- ○ 2 ripe mangoes, diced
- ○ 1 red bell pepper, diced
- ○ 1/2 red onion, diced
- ○ 1 chili pepper, seeded and minced
- ○ 1 lime, juiced
- ○ 2 tbsp fresh cilantro, chopped

Method

1. Preheat the grill to medium-high heat.
2. Season chicken breasts with salt and pepper, and brush with olive oil.
3. Grill chicken for 6-8 minutes per side or until cooked through.
4. While the chicken is cooking, prepare the mango salsa by combining mango, red bell pepper, red onion, chili pepper, lime juice, and cilantro in a bowl.
5. Season with salt and pepper to taste.
6. Once the chicken is cooked, remove it from the grill and let rest for 5 minutes.
7. Serve chicken topped with mango salsa.

Nutrition: 1 serving / whole meal, calories 268 / 1074, protein(g) 26 / 104, carbs(g) 8 / 34, fats(g) 14 / 58, fiber(g) 1 / 6, sodium(mg) 43 / 175, sugar(g) 6 / 24, saturated fat(g) 2 / 10

Pesto Zucchini Noodles

4 servings

Prep: 10 min | Cook: 10 min | Total: 20 min

Ingredients

- ○ 4 medium zucchinis, spiralized
- ○ 1 cup of fresh basil leaves
- ○ 1/4 cup of pine nuts
- ○ 1/4 cup of grated parmesan cheese
- ○ 2 garlic cloves
- ○ 1/4 cup of olive oil
- ○ Salt and pepper, to taste

Method

1. Add the basil, pine nuts, garlic, parmesan cheese, salt, and pepper to a food processor. Pulse until everything is chopped.

2. While the food processor is running, slowly add in the olive oil until the pesto is fully combined.

3. In a large pan over medium heat, add the zucchini noodles and cook until they start to soften about 5 minutes.

4. Add the pesto sauce to the pan and toss until the noodles are fully coated and heated through.

5. Serve immediately and enjoy!

Nutrition: 1 serving / whole meal, calories 209 / 837, protein(g) 6 / 27, carbs(g) 5 / 22, fats(g) 19 / 78, fiber(g) 1 / 6, sodium(mg) 59 / 239, sugar(g) 1 / 6, saturated fat(g) 3 / 12

Baked Turkey Meatballs
4 servings

Prep: 15 min | Cook: 25 min | Total: 40 min

Ingredients

- ○ 1 lb ground turkey (500g)
- ○ 1/2 cup seasoned bread crumbs
- ○ 1/4 cup grated Parmesan cheese
- ○ 1/4 cup chopped fresh parsley
- ○ 1 medium egg
- ○ 1 garlic clove, minced
- ○ Salt and pepper
- ○ 1 can of tomato sauce (15oz/400g)
- ○ 1/4 cup shredded mozzarella cheese

Method

1. Preheat the oven to 375°F (190°C).
2. In a large bowl, mix the ground turkey, breadcrumbs, Parmesan cheese, parsley, egg, garlic, salt, and pepper.
3. Form the mixture into 16 meatballs.
4. Place meatballs in a 9x13-inch baking dish and pour tomato sauce over them.
5. Bake for 20 minutes, then sprinkle mozzarella cheese on top and bake for an additional 5 minutes or until the cheese is melted and bubbly.

Nutrition: 1 serving / whole meal, calories 296 / 1187, protein(g) 29 / 118, carbs(g) 16 / 64, fats(g) 12 / 51, fiber(g) 1 / 7, sodium(mg) 636 / 2546, sugar(g) 4 / 18, saturated fat(g) 4 / 17

Spaghetti with Garlic
4 servings

Prep: 10 min | Cook: 20 min | Total: 30 min

Ingredients

- ○ 1 lbs whole wheat spaghetti (450g)
- ○ 4 cloves garlic, minced
- ○ 4 tbsp olive oil
- ○ 2 tbsp fresh parsley, chopped
- ○ 1 tsp salt
- ○ 1/4 tsp black pepper

Method

1. Bring a large pot of salted water to a boil.
2. Add the spaghetti and cook according to package instructions.
3. Heat the olive oil in a large skillet over medium heat.
4. Add the garlic and cook until fragrant, about 1 minute.
5. Drain the cooked spaghetti and add it to the skillet with the garlic and oil.
6. Stir in the parsley, salt, and pepper.
7. Stir the spaghetti and garlic mixture until everything is combined and heated through, about 2 minutes.
8. Serve hot.

Nutrition: 1 serving / whole meal, calories 496 / 1986, protein(g) 10 / 42, carbs(g) 82 / 328, fats(g) 14 / 56, fiber(g) 3 / 12, sodium(mg) 234 / 938, sugar(g) 2 / 8, saturated fat(g) 2 / 8

Spaghetti w/ Mushrooms

4 servings

Prep: 10 min | Cook: 20 min | Total: 30 min

Ingredients

- ○ 1 lbs whole wheat spaghetti (0.45 kg)
- ○ 2 tbsp olive oil
- ○ 2 garlic cloves, minced
- ○ 1 large onion, chopped
- ○ 0.5 lbs mushrooms, sliced (250 g)
- ○ 0.5 lbs spinach (250 g)
- ○ Salt and pepper, to taste
- ○ 1 tbsp parmesan cheese, grated (optional)

Method

1. Boil the spaghetti according to the instructions on the packet.
2. Heat the olive oil in a large pan over medium heat.
3. Add the garlic, onion, and mushrooms. Cook until onions are soft and mushrooms are golden.
4. Add the spinach and cook until wilted.
5. Drain the spaghetti and add it to the pan. Mix and season with salt and pepper.
6. Divide the spaghetti among the plates.
7. Top with grated Parmesan cheese.

Nutrition: 1 serving / whole meal, calories 406 / 1624, protein(g) 12 / 50, carbs(g) 58 / 232, fats(g) 14 / 56, fiber(g) 7 / 28, sodium(mg) 201 / 806, sugar(g) 3 / 15, saturated fat(g) 2 / 8

Mediterranean Spaghetti
4 servings

Prep: 10 min | Cook: 10 min | Total: 20 min

Ingredients

- ◯ 1 lb whole wheat spaghetti (450 g)
- ◯ 2 tbsp olive oil
- ◯ 3 cloves of garlic, minced
- ◯ 1 red onion, diced
- ◯ 1/4 cup white wine
- ◯ 1/4 cup olives, pitted and halved
- ◯ 4 medium tomatoes, sliced, or 1 can of sliced tomatoes
- ◯ A pinch of salt and black pepper
- ◯ 1/4 cup fresh parsley, chopped
- ◯ 1/4 cup Parmesan cheese, grated (100g)

Method

1. Bring a large pot of salted water to a boil.
2. Add the spaghetti and cook according to package instructions until al dente.
3. Meanwhile, heat the olive oil in a large skillet set over medium heat.
4. Add the garlic, onion and cook until the onion is softened and lightly browned, about 5 minutes.
5. Add the white wine and cook for 2 minutes.
6. Drain the spaghetti, reserving 1/2 cup of the cooking water.
7. Add the spaghetti to the skillet, along with the reserved cooking water.
8. Add the olives, tomatoes, salt, and pepper and toss to coat.
9. Cook for 2 minutes, stirring occasionally.
10. Remove the skillet from the heat and add the parsley and Parmesan.
11. Toss well to combine.
12. Serve immediately.

Nutrition: 1 serving / whole meal, calories 504 / 2018, protein(g) 16 / 67, carbs(g) 74 / 297, fats(g) 13 / 53, fiber(g) 7 / 28, sodium(mg) 386 / 1544, sugar(g) 8 / 32, saturated fat(g) 3 / 13

Shrimp Spaghetti

4 servings

Prep: 10 min | Cook: 10 min | Total: 20 min

Ingredients

- ○ 1 lb whole wheat spaghetti (450g)
- ○ 2 tbsp olive oil
- ○ 1 small onion, diced
- ○ 1 garlic clove, minced
- ○ 0.5 lbs cherry tomatoes, sliced (250 g)
- ○ 1/2 lb of raw shrimp, peeled and deveined (500 g)
- ○ 1/4 tsp red pepper flakes
- ○ 2 tsp fresh lemon juice
- ○ A pinch of salt and black pepper
- ○ 1/4 cup fresh parsley, chopped
- ○ 1/4 cup Parmesan cheese, grated 100 g (optional)

Method

1. Bring a large pot of salted water to a boil.
2. Add the spaghetti and cook according to package instructions until ready.
3. Meanwhile, heat the olive oil in a large skillet set over medium heat.
4. Add the onion and garlic, and cook until the onion is softened (about 5 minutes).
5. Add the shrimp, tomatoes, red pepper flakes, lemon juice, salt, and pepper, and cook until the shrimp are pink and cooked through about 2 minutes.
6. Drain the spaghetti, reserving 1/2 cup of the cooking water.
7. Add the spaghetti to the skillet, along with the reserved cooking water.
8. Toss to combine.
9. Remove the skillet from the heat and add the parsley and Parmesan cheese.
10. Serve immediately.

Nutrition: 1 serving / whole meal, calories 421 / 1686, protein(g) 22 / 90, carbs(g) 54 / 217, fats(g) 11 / 46, fiber(g) 4 / 16, sodium(mg) 277 / 1109, sugar(g) 3 / 15, saturated fat(g) 3 / 12

Oatmeal with Banana

1 serving

Prep: 5 min | Cook: 10 min | Total: 15 min

Ingredients

- ○ ½ cup rolled oats (40 g)
- ○ 1 cup milk of your choice (240 ml)
- ○ 1 medium banana, mashed
- ○ 2 tbsp walnuts, chopped
- ○ 1 tsp cinnamon
- ○ 1 tbsp honey

Method

1. Combine the oats and milk in a small saucepan and bring to a boil.
2. Reduce the heat to low and simmer for about 5 minutes or until the oats are cooked.
3. Stir in the mashed banana and walnuts.
4. Add the cinnamon and honey.
5. Increase the heat to medium and simmer for another 5 minutes, stirring frequently.
6. Serve warm.

Nutrition: 1 serving / whole meal, calories 436 / 436, protein(g) 14 / 14, carbs(g) 61 / 61, fats(g) 16 / 16, fiber(g) 7 / 7, sodium(mg) 96 / 96, sugar(g) 27 / 27, saturated fat(g) 2 / 2

Spinach Salad

2 servings

Prep: 5 min | Cook: 10 min | Total: 15 min

Ingredients

- ○ 2 medium-boiled eggs
- ○ 1 can of green beans (14.5 oz / 400g)
- ○ 1 can of mushrooms (4 oz / 100g)
- ○ 1 ½ cups of chopped spinach (45g)
- ○ 1 small head of onion (optional)
- ○ 2-3 pinches of chopped parsley
- ○ Salt by taste

Method

1. Add some water and boil the eggs for about 7-10 minutes until ready.
2. Meanwhile, wash and cut into small pieces the spinach, onion, and parsley and place them in a big bowl.
3. Once the egg is ready, put it in cold water, peel it, and cut it into small pieces in the bowl.
4. Drain the liquid from both cans and add the mushrooms and green beans in the bowl.
5. Add salt, olive oil and mix everything well.
6. Split into equal portions.

Nutrition: 1 serving / whole meal, calories 209 / 419, protein(g) 12 / 24, carbs(g) 12 / 25, fats(g) 14 / 28, fiber(g) 5 / 11, sodium(mg) 281 / 563, sugar(g) 3 / 7, saturated fat(g) 3 / 6

Salmon Salad

2 servings

Prep: 10 min | Cook: 5 min | Total: 15 min

Ingredients

- ○ 1 small head of lettuce
- ○ 1 medium tomato
- ○ 1 medium cucumber
- ○ 7.5 oz canned salmon fillets (240g)
- ○ 1 tbsp of wine vinegar
- ○ 1 tbsp of balsamic vinegar
- ○ 1 tbsp olive oil
- ○ Salt by taste

Method

1. Wash, peel and cut the tomatoes, lettuce, and cucumber in small pieces in a big bowl.
2. Add the drained salmon fillets. (cut them if needed)
3. Taste with olive oil, both kinds of vinegar, and salt.
4. Mix everything well.
5. Split into equal portions, with similar amounts of salmon per portion.

Nutrition: 1 serving / whole meal, calories 176 / 352, protein(g) 18 / 36, carbs(g) 5 / 10, fats(g) 9 / 19, fiber(g) 2 / 4, sodium(mg) 300 / 601, sugar(g) 2 / 4, saturated fat(g) 1 / 3

French Carrot Salad

4 servings

Prep: 5 min | Cook: 10 min | Total: 15 min

Ingredients

- ○ 1 pound carrots, peeled (500g)
- ○ 2 tsp Dijon mustard
- ○ 1 tsp freshly squeezed lemon juice, from one lemon
- ○ 1½ tsp extra virgin olive oil
- ○ 1-2 tsps honey, to taste
- ○ Salt and black pepper by taste
- ○ 2 tbsps chopped fresh parsley
- ○ 2 finely sliced scallions (or 1tbsp finely chopped shallots)

Method

1. Grate the carrots using a food processor or a box grater.
2. In a small bowl, whisk together the Dijon mustard, lemon juice, olive oil, honey, salt, and black pepper to make the dressing.
3. Add the dressing to the grated carrots and toss to combine.
4. Add the chopped parsley and sliced scallions, and toss again.
5. Serve chilled or at room temperature.
6. Note: This salad is best served chilled and can be made ahead of time. To make it a day in advance, prepare the salad and store it in the refrigerator until you are ready to serve.

Nutrition: 1 serving / whole meal, calories 65 / 263, protein(g) 0 / 3, carbs(g) 8 / 34, fats(g) 3 / 14, fiber(g) 2 / 9, sodium(mg) 86 / 347, sugar(g) 4 / 18, saturated fat(g) 0 / 2

Chicken Salad

4 servings

Prep: 10 min | Cook: 20 min | Total: 30 min

Ingredients

- ○ 1 medium head of iceberg lettuce
- ○ 1 lb of chicken breast (500g)
- ○ 2 tbsp olive oil
- ○ 0.5 lbs cherry tomatoes (250 g)
- ○ 1 tbsp lemon juice (optional)
- ○ 1 tbsp garlic sauce (optional)
- ○ Salt and black pepper by taste

Method

1. Cut the meat in small pieces, add salt and black pepper and mix it well.
2. Cook the breast in a large pan on medium heat with a bit of olive oil until all sides are ready. (Keep turning them over regularly)
3. Wash the tomatoes and lettuce (remove all the leaves before washing) and cut them into small pieces in a big bowl.
4. Once the chicken meat is ready, add it to the salad.
5. Add the olive oil, wine vinegar, and salt, and mix well. Add the garlic sauce on top.
6. Split into equal portions and leave in the fridge once the meat is cooled down if needed.

Nutrition: 1 serving / whole meal, calories 201 / 805, protein(g) 25 / 102, carbs(g) 4 / 16, fats(g) 8 / 35, fiber(g) 1 / 6, sodium(mg) 48 / 193, sugar(g) 2 / 8, saturated fat(g) 1 / 5

Shopska Salad

2 servings

Prep: 10 min | Cook: 0 min | Total: 10 min

Method

1. Wash, peel and cut the onion, tomatoes, cucumber, peppers (without the seeds) and the olives (without the bones) in a big bowl.

2. Add the olive oil, wine vinegar, and salt by taste and mix everything well.

3. Grate the tofu cheese on top. (Optionally add a couple of whole olives on top).

Ingredients

○ 2 medium tomatoes
○ 1 large cucumber or 2 small ones
○ 2 medium red or green bell peppers
○ 5 tbsp tofu / ½ cup feta cheese (100g)
○ 1 medium head of onion (160g)
○ 2 tbsp olive oil
○ 5 black olives
○ 1 tbsp of wine vinegar (optional)
○ Salt (by taste)

Nutrition: 1 serving / whole meal, calories 197 / 394, protein(g) 6 / 12, carbs(g) 14 / 28, fats(g) 14 / 28, fiber(g) 4 / 8, sodium(mg) 266 / 532, sugar(g) 5 / 11, saturated fat(g) 2 / 4

Cod Fish Salad
1 serving

Prep: 5 min | Cook: 10 min | Total: 15 min

Ingredients

- ○ 4.2 oz canned codfish (120g)
- ○ 2 medium tomatoes
- ○ 1 medium head of onion
- ○ 1 large egg
- ○ 1 tbsp olive oil
- ○ 5 lettuce leaves
- ○ 1/2 cups Parmesan cheese, grated (50 g) (optional)
- ○ 1/2 cups croutons (50 g) (optional)
- ○ Salt (by taste)

Method

1. Put the egg in water and boil it for 7-10 minutes.
2. Meanwhile, wash, peel and cut the onion, tomatoes, and lettuce into small pieces and add them inside a big bowl.
3. Drain the can, cut the codfish into small pieces, and add it inside the bowl.
4. Once the egg is ready, peel it and cut it into medium pieces and add them to the bowl.
5. Add the olive oil, wine vinegar, and salt. Mix well.
6. Finish with the Parmesan cheese and the croutons.

Nutrition: 1 serving / whole meal, calories 525 / 525, protein(g) 36 / 36, carbs(g) 16 / 16, fats(g) 37 / 37, fiber(g) 3 / 3, sodium(mg) 1035 / 1035, sugar(g) 5 / 5, saturated fat(g) 12 / 12

Avocado Salad
2 servings

Prep: 5 min | Cook: 5 min | Total: 10 min

Method

1. Wash well the vegetables.
2. Grate the carrots and cabbage in thin lines and place them in a large bowl.
3. Cut everything else into small equal pieces and place them in the bowl. (You can optionally peel the cucumber)
4. Add the olive oil, wine vinegar, and salt.
5. Mix well and eat while fresh.

Ingredients

- ○ 1 average avocado
- ○ 1 large tomato
- ○ 1 small onion head, chopped
- ○ 2 medium carrots, grated
- ○ 0.5 lbs cabbage (250g), grated
- ○ 1 tbsp olive oil
- ○ 1 tbsp wine vinegar
- ○ Salt (by taste)

Nutrition: 1 serving / whole meal, calories 265 / 530, protein(g) 4 / 9, carbs(g) 22 / 44, fats(g) 20 / 40, fiber(g) 10 / 20, sodium(mg) 212 / 424, sugar(g) 5 / 11, saturated fat(g) 2 / 5

Cabbage Salad

1 serving

Prep: 10 min | Cook: 5 min | Total: 15 min

Method

1. Wash, peel and grate the carrots and cabbage into small pieces inside a large bowl.

2. Wash and chop into small pieces the parsley and fennel and add them inside the bowl.

3. Add the olive oil, wine vinegar, and salt.

4. Mix well and eat while fresh. You can combine this salad with some type of meat or protein-rich dish.

Ingredients

- ○ 1 lb/half large cabbage head (500g)
- ○ 3 medium carrots
- ○ 2-3 stalks of fennel (optional)
- ○ 2-3 stalks of parsley (optional)
- ○ 1 tbsp olive oil
- ○ 1 tbsp wine vinegar (optional)
- ○ Salt (by taste)

Nutrition: 1 serving / whole meal, calories 165 / 165, protein(g) 4 / 4, carbs(g) 28 / 28, fats(g) 6 / 6, fiber(g) 12 / 12, sodium(mg) 106 / 106, sugar(g) 16 / 16, saturated fat(g) 1 / 1

Broccoli Salad

1 serving

Prep: 5 min | Cook: 15 min | Total: 20 min

Ingredients

- ○ 0.5 lbs/ half large head of broccoli (250g)
- ○ 3 medium carrots, chopped
- ○ 1 small head of onion, chopped
- ○ 1 medium lemon (optional)
- ○ 2 tbsp olive oil
- ○ Salt (by taste)
- ○ 1 pinch chopped red-hot pepper (optional)

Method

1. Wash well and split the broccoli into the shape of small flowers.
2. Wash, peel, and cut the carrots and onion into small pieces.
3. Add everything inside a large pot and fill it with enough water, so they are under it. Put the pot on high heat and boil everything for 3 minutes.
4. Remove the veggies from the pot, and rinse them with cold water in a strainer.
5. Next, steam the broccoli in a pan with a lid on with olive oil, and 3 tbsp of water for 8-10 minutes everything is soft on medium heat.
6. Transfer everything to a plate, and add lemon juice and salt.
7. Serve with a protein-rich dish.

Nutrition: 1 serving / whole meal, calories 255 / 255, protein(g) 7 / 7, carbs(g) 26 / 26, fats(g) 16 / 16, fiber(g) 11 / 11, sodium(mg) 167 / 167, sugar(g) 8 / 8, saturated fat(g) 2 / 2

Quinoa Salad

3 servings

Prep: 10 min | Cook: 20 min | Total: 30 min

Ingredients

- ○ 1 cup quinoa (170 g)
- ○ 2 cups of water (2:1 ratio)
- ○ 1 lb cherry tomatoes (500 g) / Regular (alternative)
- ○ 1 large cucumber
- ○ 2 tbsp olive oil
- ○ Salt by taste

Method

1. In a large enough pot boil 2 cups of water on high heat.
2. Drain the quinoa with cold water and once the water starts to boil add it carefully to the pot, put the lid on, lower the heat to low and leave simmering for 15 min. Then turn off the heat and leave the lid on for 5 minutes.
3. Meanwhile wash the vegetables, cut the ends of the cucumber, peel it and cut it into small pieces. Add them in a big bowl.
4. Cut each cherry tomato in half (or leave them whole) and place them in the bowl.
5. Once the quinoa is ready, slowly add it to the bowl.
6. Pour on top the olive oil, add the salt, and mix everything well.
7. Split into 3 equal portions and store rest in fringe for 3-4 days.

Nutrition: 1 serving / whole meal, calories 338 / 1015, protein(g) 8 / 26, carbs(g) 51 / 154, fats(g) 11 / 33, fiber(g) 8 / 26, sodium(mg) 40 / 122, sugar(g) 5 / 16, saturated fat(g) 1 / 4

Tomato Salad

2 servings

Prep: 15 min | Cook: 0 min | Total: 15 min

Ingredients

- ○ 1 medium head of lettuce
- ○ 4 medium tomatoes (800g)
- ○ 4-5 raw turnips
- ○ 2 tbsp olive oil
- ○ Salt by taste

Method

1. Wash all the vegetables well with warm water.
2. Remove the pedicels and slice the tomatoes into medium pieces and place them in a big bowl.
3. Remove the leaves and cut the turnips into small pieces. Place them in the same bowl.
4. Separate the lettuce leaves, stack them a few at a time, and cut them in thin lines. Place them inside a large bowl separately.
5. Once ready, mix the chopped veggies with the lettuce in the big bowl.
6. Pour the olive oil and add salt by taste.
7. Mix everything well and separate the salad into 2 equal portions.

Nutrition: 1 serving / whole meal, calories 123 / 247, protein(g) 3 / 7, carbs(g) 13 / 27, fats(g) 7 / 15, fiber(g) 5 / 11, sodium(mg) 196 / 393, sugar(g) 7 / 14, saturated fat(g) 1 / 2

Cucumber & Avocado Salad

2 servings

Prep: 10 min | Cook: 0 min | Total: 10 min

Ingredients

- ○ 1 large cucumber, peeled, seeded and diced
- ○ 1 medium avocado, diced
- ○ 1/4 cup diced red onion
- ○ 0.5 lbs cherry tomatoes (250g)
- ○ 1 bell pepper (red)
- ○ A couple of arugula leaves
- ○ 2 tbsp olive oil
- ○ 2 tbsp fresh lemon juice
- ○ 2 tbsp chopped fresh cilantro
- ○ 1/2 tsp garlic powder
- ○ 1/4 tsp salt
- ○ 1/4 tsp ground black pepper

Method

1. Wash and chop all the ingredients into small pieces.
2. In a medium bowl, combine the cucumber, avocado, onion, olive oil, lemon juice, cilantro, garlic powder, salt, and pepper.
3. Toss gently to combine and serve.

Nutrition: 1 serving / whole meal, calories 307 / 615, protein(g) 5 / 11, carbs(g) 20 / 41, fats(g) 25 / 50, fiber(g) 10 / 20, sodium(mg) 160 / 321, sugar(g) 6 / 12, saturated fat(g) 3 / 7

Forest Fruit Salad
1 serving

Prep: 10 min | Cook: 0 min | Total: 10 min

Ingredients

- ○ 2 cups mixed forest fruits (strawberries, raspberries, blueberries, etc.)
- ○ 1 banana, sliced
- ○ 1/4 cup fresh mint leaves, chopped
- ○ 1 tbsp honey
- ○ 1 tbsp lime juice

Method

1. Wash and prepare the fruits. Slice the banana and chop the mint leaves.
2. In a small bowl, mix together the honey and lime juice.
3. In a large bowl, combine the forest fruits, sliced banana, and chopped mint leaves.
4. Drizzle the honey-lime mixture over the fruit mixture and toss gently to coat.
5. Serve the salad chilled.

Nutrition: 1 serving / whole meal, calories 226 / 226, protein(g) 3 / 3, carbs(g) 58 / 58, fats(g) 1 / 1, fiber(g) 10 / 10, sodium(mg) 3 / 3, sugar(g) 39 / 39, saturated fat(g) 0 / 0

Greek Salad

1 serving

Prep: 10 min | Cook: 0 min | Total: 10 min

Ingredients

- ○ 1 large cucumber, chopped
- ○ 1 large tomato, chopped
- ○ 1/4 cup pitted Kalamata olives
- ○ 1/4 cup red onion, chopped
- ○ 1/4 cup feta cheese (100g)
- ○ 3 tbsp extra-virgin olive oil
- ○ 1 tsp dried oregano
- ○ 1/2 tsp garlic powder
- ○ 1/4 tsp salt
- ○ 1/4 tsp black pepper
- ○ A few arugula leaves (optional)

Method

1. Wash and chop all the ingredients into small pieces.
2. In a large bowl, combine cucumber, tomato, olives, red onion, and feta cheese.
3. In a small bowl, whisk together olive oil, oregano, garlic powder, salt, and pepper.
4. Pour the dressing over the salad and toss to combine.

Nutrition: 1 serving / whole meal, calories 464 / 464, protein(g) 13 / 13, carbs(g) 13 / 13, fats(g) 41 / 41, fiber(g) 3 / 3, sodium(mg) 1202 / 1202, sugar(g) 5 / 5, saturated fat(g) 12 / 12

Mediterranean Chopped Salad

4 servings

Prep: 15 min | Cook: 0 min | Total: 15 min

Method

1. In a large bowl, combine the cucumber, tomato, olives, feta cheese, red onion, and parsley.

2. In a small bowl, whisk together olive oil, red wine vinegar, garlic powder, oregano, and salt and pepper.

3. Pour dressing over the salad, and toss to combine.

4. Enjoy!

Ingredients

- ○ 1 large cucumber, diced
- ○ 1 large tomato, diced
- ○ 1/2 cup pitted Kalamata olives, diced
- ○ 1/4 cup feta cheese, crumbled
- ○ 1/4 cup red onion, diced
- ○ 1/4 cup fresh parsley, chopped
- ○ 1/4 cup extra-virgin olive oil
- ○ 2 tbsp red wine vinegar
- ○ 1 tsp garlic powder
- ○ 1/2 tsp oregano
- ○ Salt and black pepper, to taste

Nutrition: 1 serving / whole meal, calories 190 / 760, protein(g) 4 / 17, carbs(g) 4 / 18, fats(g) 18 / 72, fiber(g) 1 / 6, sodium(mg) 242 / 970, sugar(g) 1 / 4, saturated fat(g) 5 / 20

Caprese Salad

4 servings

Prep: 10 min | Cook: 0 min | Total: 10 min

Method

1. In a large bowl, combine the tomatoes, mozzarella cheese, olives, olive oil, balsamic vinegar, garlic, garlic powder, oregano, and basil.

2. Mix until all ingredients are well incorporated.

3. Season with salt and pepper, to taste.

4. Serve immediately while fresh.

Ingredients

- ○ 2 large tomatoes, diced
- ○ 1/2 cup mozzarella cheese, cubed
- ○ 1/4 cup olives, pitted and halved
- ○ 1 tsp olive oil
- ○ 2 tbsp balsamic vinegar
- ○ 2 cloves garlic, minced
- ○ 1/4 tsp garlic powder
- ○ 1/4 tsp oregano
- ○ 1/4 tsp basil
- ○ Salt and pepper, to taste

Nutrition: 1 serving / whole meal, calories 71 / 286, protein(g) 3 / 14, carbs(g) 2 / 11, fats(g) 5 / 22, fiber(g) 0 / 3, sodium(mg) 139 / 559, sugar(g) 0 / 3, saturated fat(g) 1 / 7

Quinoa & Tomato Salad
3 servings

Prep: 5 min | Cook: 20 min | Total: 25 min

Ingredients

- ○ 2 cups quinoa (380g)
- ○ 1 cup arugula
- ○ 0.2 lbs radishes (100g)
- ○ 0.5 lbs cherry tomatoes (250g)
- ○ 1 medium cucumber
- ○ 2 tbsp olive oil
- ○ 1 tbsp freshly squeezed lime juice (optional)
- ○ 1 pinch chia seeds (optional)
- ○ Salt and black pepper by taste

Method

1. In a large enough pot boil 4 cups of water on high heat.

2. Drain the quinoa with cold water and once the water starts to boil add it carefully to the pot, put the lid on, lower the heat to low and leave simmering for 15 min. Then turn off the heat and leave the lid on for 5 more minutes. (2:1 ratio, 2 cups quinoa = 4 cups of water)

3. Meanwhile, wash and chop all the vegetables and place them in a large bowl.

4. Once the quinoa is ready add it to the bowl, pour the olive oil and spices on top, and mix everything together.

5. Split into 3 portions and eat while fresh!

Nutrition: 1 serving / whole meal, calories 425 / 1275, protein(g) 10 / 31, carbs(g) 59 / 177, fats(g) 17 / 51, fiber(g) 11 / 33, sodium(mg) 16 / 50, sugar(g) 4 / 13, saturated fat(g) 2 / 7

Strawberry & Cherry Salad
1 serving

Prep: 10 min | Cook: 0 min | Total: 10 min

Ingredients

- ○ 1 cup strawberries, sliced (160g)
- ○ 1 cup cherries, pitted and halved (20 cherries)
- ○ 1/4 cup chopped almonds
- ○ 1/4 cup plain Greek yogurt
- ○ A handful of strawberries
- ○ 2 medium bananas
- ○ 1 tbsp honey

Method

1. Blend together the Greek yogurt, with the strawberries and bananas until liquid.
2. In a large salad bowl, combine the mixed greens, sliced strawberries, and halved cherries.
3. Drizzle the dressing over the salad and toss to combine.
4. Sprinkle the chopped almonds on top of the salad before serving.

Nutrition: 1 serving / whole meal, calories 557 / 557, protein(g) 17 / 17, carbs(g) 89 / 89, fats(g) 17 / 17, fiber(g) 12 / 12, sodium(mg) 43 / 43, sugar(g) 62 / 62, saturated fat(g) 2 / 2

Mexican Mix Salad

2 servings

Prep: 15 min | Cook: 0 min | Total: 15 min

Method

1. Wash well and chop the tomato and white onion in small pieces and place them in a large bowl.

2. Add the drained green beans (slice if needed), red kidney beans, peas, and sweet corn to the bowl.

3. Add the olive oil and spices on top and mix everything together.

4. Split into 2 portions and eat while fresh!

Ingredients

- ◯ 1 large tomato, sliced
- ◯ 1 cup drained canned green beans (15oz/400g)
- ◯ ½ cup of drained canned red kidney beans (8oz/200g)
- ◯ ¼ cup of sweet corn (65g) (frozen is preferred)
- ◯ 1 small head of white onion, chopped
- ◯ ½ cup of drained canned peas
- ◯ 2 tbsp olive oil
- ◯ Salt by taste
- ◯ Black pepper by taste

Nutrition: 1 serving / whole meal, calories 250 / 500, protein(g) 8 / 17, carbs(g) 30 / 61, fats(g) 11 / 22, fiber(g) 9 / 19, sodium(mg) 502 / 1005, sugar(g) 5 / 11, saturated fat(g) 1 / 3

Tomato & Spinach Salad

1 serving

Prep: 15 min | Cook: 0 min | Total: 15 min

Method

1. Wash and chop all the spinach and tomatoes in small pieces and place them in a large bowl.
2. Peel and grate the carrots in thin lines.
3. Add them to the bowl, pour the olive oil and spices on top, and mix everything together.
4. Split in 2 portions and eat while fresh!

Ingredients

- ○ 0.5 lbs spinach, chopped (250g)
- ○ 0.5 lbs cherry tomatoes (250g)
- ○ 2 medium carrots, grated
- ○ ¼ cup of sweet corn (65g) (frozen is preferred)
- ○ 2 tbsp olive oil
- ○ Salt by taste
- ○ Black pepper

Nutrition: 1 serving / whole meal, calories 430 / 430, protein(g) 13 / 13, carbs(g) 35 / 35, fats(g) 30 / 30, fiber(g) 11 / 11, sodium(mg) 416 / 416, sugar(g) 10 / 10, saturated fat(g) 4 / 4

Bean Soup

3 servings

Prep: 10 min | Cook: 1 h 0 min | Total: 1 h 10 min

Ingredients

○ 2 cups of raw white kidney beans (or 15oz can of white beans (400 g)

○ 4 medium carrots

○ 4 medium onions

○ 4 and 1/4 cups of water (1 liter)

○ 3 pinches of spearmint

○ Salt by taste

○ 1 tbsp paprika

Method

1. Wash the beans well in a strainer. (If we use can drain it)

2. In a big pot on high heat, add all the water and then insert the beans and wait for it to start boiling.

3. Meanwhile, wash, peel, and cut the onions and carrots into small pieces and add them to the pot.

4. Add all the spices and mix everything well.

5. Once it starts boiling, turn down the heat to medium and boil for around 1 hour if the beans are raw. If not, boil until the carrots and onion get soft and ready.

6. Once ready, remove the pot from heat, wait for it to cool down, and separate the meal into equal portions.

Nutrition: 1 serving / whole meal, calories 381 / 1145, protein(g) 18 / 54, carbs(g) 75 / 226, fats(g) 1 / 4, fiber(g) 19 / 58, sodium(mg) 103 / 310, sugar(g) 9 / 27, saturated fat(g) 0 / 1

Fish Soup

4 servings

Prep: 10 min | Cook: 30 min | Total: 40 min

Ingredients

- ○ 1 lb tuna filet (500g)
- ○ 3 tbsp olive oil
- ○ 1 medium head of onion
- ○ 4 medium tomatoes or 1 can dice tomatoes (14.5 oz) (400g)
- ○ 1/2 medium lemon
- ○ 1 cup of chopped parsley
- ○ 8 cups and 1/2 of water (2 liters)
- ○ Salt (by taste)
- ○ Black pepper (by taste)

Method

1. Cut the tuna filet into small pieces and set aside.

2. Wash, peel, and cut the onion, tomatoes (if whole), and parsley into small pieces and cubes. (place the parsley in a separate container)

3. In a big pot add all the water, olive oil, and salt and put the lid on until it starts boiling on high heat.

4. Then gently add the onion and tomatoes, lower the heat to medium, and boil for 15 more minutes.

5. Add gently the fish and, lower the heat to low, put the lid on and boil until ready. (You should be able to split the meat with a fork easily)

6. Finally, remove from the stove, add all the spices, lemon juice and sprinkle the chopped parsley and mix everything well. Split into equal portions.

Nutrition: 1 serving / whole meal, calories 437 / 1750, protein(g) 48 / 195, carbs(g) 9 / 36, fats(g) 21 / 87, fiber(g) 2 / 9, sodium(mg) 343 / 1375, sugar(g) 3 / 15, saturated fat(g) 3 / 12

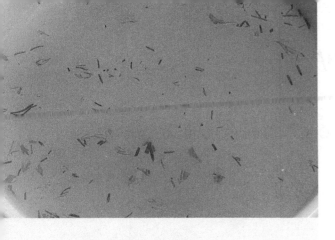

Chicken Soup
2 servings

Prep: 10 min | Cook: 40 min | Total: 50 min

Ingredients

- ○ 0.7 lbs of chicken breast (350g)
- ○ 2 medium carrots
- ○ 1 medium head of onion
- ○ 2 tbsp olive oil
- ○ 2 medium lemons (optional)
- ○ 6 cups and 1/2 of water (1.5 liters)
- ○ Salt (by taste)
- ○ Black pepper (by taste) (optional)
- ○ Paprika (by taste) (optional)

Method

1. Cut the chicken breast into small pieces (2-3 inches/5-8 cm) and set aside.
2. Wash, peel, and cut the onion and the carrots into small pieces and cubes.
3. In a big pot add all the water, olive oil, and salt and put the lid on until it starts boiling on high heat.
4. Then gently add the meat, lower the heat to medium, and boil until the meat is ready. (it is done when you can easily break it with a fork).
5. After the meat is ready, add the vegetables and all the spices, mix well, lower the heat to low with the lid on, and leave on the stove until the carrots are soft and done.
6. Once it's cooled down a bit, you can optionally add lemon juice for extra flavor. Split into equal portions.

Nutrition: 1 serving / whole meal, calories 300 / 600, protein(g) 49 / 98, carbs(g) 7 / 14, fats(g) 7 / 15, fiber(g) 1 / 3, sodium(mg) 157 / 315, sugar(g) 3 / 7, saturated fat(g) 1 / 2

Mushroom Soup
3 servings

Prep: 10 min | Cook: 40 min | Total: 50 min

Ingredients

- ○ 1 lb of mushrooms (any) (500 g)
- ○ 1/2 cup of raw brown rice (100 g)
- ○ 1 medium carrot
- ○ 1 medium head of onion
- ○ 2 tbsp olive oil
- ○ 6 and 1/2 cups of water (1.5 liters)
- ○ Salt (by taste)
- ○ Black pepper (by taste) (optional)

Method

1. Wash the rice well in a strainer with cold water for 1 minute.

2. Place in a big pot, all the water with, a bit of salt. Set it on high heat and wait for the water to boil. Once the water is boiling, add the rice slowly and boil it for 30 minutes. Strained the extra water and then let it rest in a bowl.

3. While the rice is boiling, wash, peel and cut into small pieces and cubes the onion and the carrots. Wash and chop the mushrooms in small pieces in a separate bowl.

4. Steam the onion and carrots in a pan with a lid on with the olive oil, and 3 tbsp of water for 8-10 minutes until they are soft on medium heat.

5. Once the carrots are soft, add the mushrooms and stir for 5 min nonstop.

6. Transfer the rice to the pan and add all the spices.

7. Mix everything well and cook for a couple of minutes.

8. Remove from heat, wait for it to cool down, and split into equally sized portions.

Nutrition: 1 serving / whole meal, calories 233 / 700, protein(g) 6 / 19, carbs(g) 35 / 105, fats(g) 9 / 27, fiber(g) 5 / 16, sodium(mg) 6 / 20, sugar(g) 4 / 14, saturated fat(g) 1 / 4

Zucchini Soup
4 servings

Prep: 10 min | Cook: 30 min | Total: 40 min

Ingredients

- ○ 2 medium green summer squash (zucchini) (400g)
- ○ 2 medium carrots (120g)
- ○ 1 medium head of onion
- ○ 2 tbsp olive oil
- ○ 6 cups and 1/2 of water (1.5 liters)
- ○ Salt (by taste)
- ○ Black pepper (by taste) (optional)

Method

1. Wash, peel and cut into small pieces and cubes the onion and the carrots.

2. Wash and cut into circles the zucchini with the skin.

3. Steam together all the vegetables in a large pan with olive oil, and 3 tbsp of water for 8-10 minutes until they are soft on medium heat.

4. Once they are ready, place everything into a big pot with all the water and let it boil until all the vegetables are fully ready and soft.

5. Finally, add all the spices by taste, mix well, remove from heat, and split into equal portions.

Nutrition: 1 serving / whole meal, calories 82 / 330, protein(g) 1 / 7, carbs(g) 6 / 26, fats(g) 5 / 23, fiber(g) 2 / 8, sodium(mg) 7 / 30, sugar(g) 3 / 14, saturated fat(g) 0 / 3

Pea Soup

6 servings

Prep: 15 min | Cook: 25 min | Total: 40 min

Method

1. Wash, peel and cut into small pieces and cubes the onion, carrots, the zucchini, and the broccoli. (separate the zucchini in a different bowl)

2. Steam the onion, carrots, and broccoli in a large pan with the olive oil, and 3 tbsp of water for 8-10 minutes until they are soft on medium heat.

3. Add the zucchini and peas and stir for 5-10 more minutes. Then add the water and stir again until all the vegetables are ready and soft.

4. Take the pan off the heat, wait to cool down, and mash and blend everything until everything is liquid.

5. Add all the spices and separate them in equal portions in bowls and meal prep.

Ingredients

- ○ 1 can of peas (drained) (15 oz / 400g)
- ○ 2 medium carrots
- ○ 1 medium head of onion
- ○ 1 medium green summer squash (zucchini) (200g)
- ○ 0.5 lbs/ half large head of broccoli (250g)
- ○ 8 cups and 1/2 of water (2 liters)
- ○ Salt (by taste)
- ○ Black pepper (by taste) (optional)

Nutrition: 1 serving / whole meal, calories 55 / 330, protein(g) 2 / 16, carbs(g) 10 / 60, fats(g) 0 / 2, fiber(g) 3 / 22, sodium(mg) 153 / 920, sugar(g) 2 / 15, saturated fat(g) 0 / 0

Tomato Soup
2 servings

Prep: 10 min | Cook: 30 min | Total: 40 min

Ingredients

- ○ 6 medium tomatoes or 4 large tomatoes
- ○ 1 medium head of onion
- ○ 2 tbsp olive oil
- ○ 1 cup of water (240 ml)
- ○ Salt (by taste)
- ○ Summer savory (optional)
- ○ 1 pinch of parsley (optional)

Method

1. Peel the onion and cut it into small pieces. (You can grate it as an alternative)

2. Steam the onion in a large pan with a lid with the olive oil and 3 tbsp of water on medium heat for 10 minutes. Stir from time to time until it is soft.

3. Meanwhile cut the tomatoes (optionally peel them) and grate everything in a large bowl.

4. Once the onion is done, add the grated tomatoes, pour the cup of water, add the salt and summer savory, stir well, and leave on medium heat for 10-15 minutes for a light boil.

5. Remove from heat, pour in a bowl, and add a pinch of parsley on top.

Nutrition: 1 serving / whole meal, calories 120 / 240, protein(g) 3 / 6, carbs(g) 15 / 30, fats(g) 7 / 14, fiber(g) 3 / 6, sodium(mg) 10 / 20, sugar(g) 9 / 18, saturated fat(g) 1 / 2

Spinach Cream Soup

1 serving

Prep: 10 min | Cook: 35 min | Total: 45 min

Method

1. Chop the onion and carrots into small pieces.
2. In a large pot, heat the olive oil over medium heat. Add the chopped onion and carrots and sauté until the onion is translucent, about 5 minutes.
3. Add the spinach and vegetable broth to the pot. Bring to a boil and let simmer for 10 minutes.
4. Remove the pot from heat and let it cool for a few minutes. Use an immersion blender or transfer the soup to a blender and puree until smooth.
5. In a small bowl, whisk together the milk and flour until smooth.
6. Return the pureed soup to the pot and bring it back to a simmer. Add the cream mixture, stirring constantly, until well combined. Simmer for an additional 5-10 minutes until the soup has thickened.
7. Season with salt and black pepper to taste. Serve hot with croutons (optional).

Ingredients

- ○ 9 oz raw spinach (250 g)
- ○ 1 medium head of onion
- ○ 2 medium carrots
- ○ 2 tbsp olive oil
- ○ 1 cup / 1 cube of vegetable broth (240 ml)
- ○ 1 cup low fat milk (240 ml)
- ○ 1 tbsp all-purpose flour
- ○ Salt (by taste)
- ○ Black pepper (by taste)

Nutrition: 1 serving / whole meal, calories 1138 / 1138, protein(g) 17 / 17, carbs(g) 51 / 51, fats(g) 98 / 98, fiber(g) 8 / 8, sodium(mg) 1379 / 1379, sugar(g) 16 / 16, saturated fat(g) 46 / 46

Red Lentil Soup
4 servings

Prep: 10 min | Cook: 40 min | Total: 50 min

Ingredients

- ○ 1 cup red lentils (200 g)
- ○ 6 cups and 1/2 of water (1.5 liters)
- ○ 1 medium head of onion
- ○ 2 medium carrots
- ○ 2 medium tomatoes or 1/2 can dice tomatoes (14.5 oz) (400g)
- ○ 2 tbsp olive oil
- ○ Mint (3 pinches) (optional)
- ○ Salt (by taste)

Method

1. Peel the onion and carrots and cut them into small cubes and pieces.

2. Pour the olive oil into a big pan with a lid (or pot) on medium heat, and place the chopped vegetables inside with 3 tbsp of water and put the lid on for 10 minutes to soften them with steam. They are ready once the carrots are soft and can be easily split in half.

3. Pour all the water into a big pot on high heat and wait for it to boil.

4. Wash the lentils using a strainer and add them to the boiling water.

5. Wash and mash the tomatoes (if whole) and add them to the lentils. Add the vegetables next, with some salt and black pepper.

6. Change the heat to low for a slow boil, put the lid almost fully on, and wait for 30-40 minutes. The lentils are ready when they are soft.

Nutrition: 1 serving / whole meal, calories 263 / 1055, protein(g) 13 / 53, carbs(g) 39 / 158, fats(g) 5 / 22, fiber(g) 13 / 52, sodium(mg) 188 / 753, sugar(g) 4 / 18, saturated fat(g) 0 / 3

Tarator

4 servings

Prep: 5 min | Cook: 5 min | Total: 10 min

Method

1. In a large bowl, mix the yogurt well with 2 cups of water.
2. Pill the cucumber and garlic and grate them together inside the mixture.
3. Add the olive oil, salt, and black pepper to taste.
4. Finely chop the fennel, sprinkle it inside, and stir well.
5. Separate them into different containers and leave them in the fridge for 2-3 hours.

Ingredients

- ○ 1 lb nonfat Greek yogurt (500g)
- ○ 1 large cucumber or 2 small ones
- ○ 1 stalk of garlic
- ○ 2-3 stalks of fennel
- ○ 2 tbsp olive oil
- ○ 2 cups of water (500 ml)
- ○ Salt (by taste)
- ○ Black pepper (by taste) (optional)

Nutrition: 1 serving / whole meal, calories 126 / 504, protein(g) 14 / 56, carbs(g) 6 / 26, fats(g) 5 / 20, fiber(g) 1 / 5, sodium(mg) 279 / 1117, sugar(g) 5 / 20, saturated fat(g) 0 / 3

Veal Broccoli Soup
5 servings

Prep: 10 min | Cook: 30 min | Total: 40 min

Ingredients

- ○ 0.8 lbs beef steak/meat (400g)
- ○ 1 medium head of onion
- ○ 0.5 lbs/ half large head of broccoli (250g)
- ○ 2 cups of chopped parsley
- ○ 1 can of drained peas (15 oz / 400g)
- ○ 4 medium carrots
- ○ 2 large stalks of celery
- ○ 1 whole medium head of garlic
- ○ 6 cups and 1/2 of water (1.5 liters)
- ○ Salt (by taste)
- ○ Black pepper (by taste) (optional)
- ○ Paprika (by taste) (optional)

Method

1. Cut the meat into small pieces, mix with salt and set aside.
2. Wash, peel, and cut the onion, celery, garlic, carrots, broccoli and parsley into small pieces and cubes.
3. In a big pot, add all the water and salt and put the lid on until it starts boiling on high heat.
4. Add the meat, lower the heat to low, and boil on a closed lid until it's ready. (You should be able to go through the meat with a fork or knife easily)
5. Once the meat is done, add all the chopped vegetables, including the peas, and stir well.
6. Leave on low heat with the lid on until all the vegetables are soft and ready.
7. Remove from the stove, add all the spices, and split into equal portions.

Nutrition: 1 serving / whole meal, calories 264 / 1323, protein(g) 24 / 123, carbs(g) 14 / 72, fats(g) 11 / 59, fiber(g) 4 / 22, sodium(mg) 211 / 1055, sugar(g) 3 / 18, saturated fat(g) 4 / 21

Creamy Avocado Soup
4 servings

Prep: 10 min | Cook: 15 min | Total: 25 min

Ingredients

- ○ 2 tbsp olive oil
- ○ 1 small onion, diced
- ○ 1 garlic clove, minced
- ○ 1 tsp cumin
- ○ 1/4 tsp black pepper
- ○ 1/4 tsp oregano
- ○ 1/4 tsp paprika
- ○ 4 cups vegetable broth (1000 ml)
- ○ 2 medium ripe avocados
- ○ 1 lime, juiced
- ○ 2 tbsp fresh cilantro

Method

1. Heat olive oil in a large pot over medium heat.
2. Add the onion, garlic and stir until soft, about 5 minutes.
3. Add the cumin, black pepper, oregano, and paprika and stir to combine.
4. Add the vegetable broth and bring to a boil.
5. Add the avocados and reduce heat to a simmer.
6. Simmer for 10 minutes, stirring occasionally.
7. Remove from heat and stir in the lime juice and cilantro.
8. Blend the soup until smooth, using an immersion blender or a standing blender.
9. Serve hot.

Nutrition: 1 serving / whole meal, calories 263 / 1053, protein(g) 3 / 15, carbs(g) 11 / 44, fats(g) 23 / 95, fiber(g) 4 / 19, sodium(mg) 416 / 1667, sugar(g) 1 / 6, saturated fat(g) 3 / 14

Broccoli & Spinach Soup

4 servings

Prep: 15 min | Cook: 15 min | Total: 30 min

Ingredients

- ○ 1 tbsp olive oil
- ○ 1/2 onion, chopped
- ○ 2 cloves garlic, minced
- ○ 1 large carrot, chopped
- ○ 1 celery stalk, chopped
- ○ 1/4 tsp ground nutmeg
- ○ 1/4 tsp ground black pepper
- ○ 1/4 tsp paprika
- ○ 3 cups vegetable broth
- ○ 2 cups broccoli florets
- ○ 2 cups baby spinach
- ○ 1 pinch of nutmeg

Method

1. Heat the oil in a large pot over medium heat. Add the onion, garlic, carrot, and celery and cook, stirring occasionally, until the vegetables are softened (about 5 minutes).

2. Add the nutmeg, black pepper, paprika, and broth, and bring to a simmer.

3. Add the broccoli and spinach, and simmer until the vegetables are tender (about 10 minutes).

4. Carefully transfer the soup to a blender and puree until smooth.

5. Serve warm.

Nutrition: 1 serving / whole meal, calories 80 / 323, protein(g) 3 / 12, carbs(g) 9 / 38, fats(g) 4 / 16, fiber(g) 2 / 11, sodium(mg) 311 / 1246, sugar(g) 2 / 9, saturated fat(g) 0 / 2

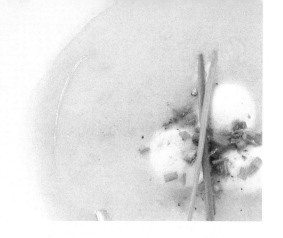

Creamy Asparagus Soup

6 servings

Prep: 10 min | Cook: 25 min | Total: 35 min

Method

1. Melt the butter in a large pot over medium heat.
2. Add the onion and garlic and cook for 5 minutes, stirring occasionally.
3. Add the asparagus and vegetable broth.
4. Bring to a boil, reduce heat, and simmer for 15 minutes.
5. Add the milk, parsley, salt, and pepper. Simmer for 5 more minutes.
6. Using an immersion blender, puree the soup until creamy.
7. Serve warm.

Ingredients

- ○ 2 tbsp butter
- ○ 1 onion, diced
- ○ 3 cloves garlic, minced
- ○ 1 lb asparagus, cut into 1-inch pieces (450g)
- ○ 3 cups vegetable broth
- ○ 2 cups milk (480ml)
- ○ 1/4 cup chopped fresh parsley
- ○ 1/2 tsp salt
- ○ 1/4 tsp black pepper

Nutrition: 1 serving / whole meal, calories 99 / 596, protein(g) 4 / 24, carbs(g) 7 / 46, fats(g) 6 / 37, fiber(g) 1 / 9, sodium(mg) 384 / 2309, sugar(g) 3 / 20, saturated fat(g) 3 / 23

Vegetable Soup

6 servings

Prep: 10 min | Cook: 25 min | Total: 35 min

Method

1. Heat the olive oil in a large pot over medium heat.
2. Add the onion, carrot, celery, and garlic and cook for 5 minutes, stirring occasionally.
3. Pour in the vegetable broth, diced tomatoes, and seasonings.
4. Bring to a boil, reduce heat, and simmer for 15 minutes.
5. Add the kidney beans and zucchini, and cook for 5 more minutes.
6. Stir in the parsley and serve.

Ingredients

- ○ 1 tbsp olive oil
- ○ 1 onion, diced
- ○ 1 medium carrot, diced
- ○ 1 large celery stalk, diced
- ○ 3 cloves garlic, minced
- ○ 6 cups vegetable broth (1.5 l)
- ○ 1 (15 oz) can dice tomatoes (400g)
- ○ 1 tsp Italian seasoning
- ○ 1/2 tsp garlic powder
- ○ 1/4 tsp black pepper
- ○ 1 (15 oz) can kidney beans, drained and rinsed (400g)
- ○ 2 medium zucchini, diced
- ○ 1/2 cup chopped fresh parsley

Nutrition: 1 serving / whole meal, calories 103 / 621, protein(g) 4 / 28, carbs(g) 16 / 99, fats(g) 2 / 12, fiber(g) 5 / 34, sodium(mg) 383 / 2302, sugar(g) 3 / 18, saturated fat(g) 0 / 2

Broccoli Soup

4 servings

Prep: 10 min | Cook: 25 min | Total: 35 min

Ingredients

- ○ 2 tbsp butter
- ○ 1 small yellow onion, diced
- ○ 2 cloves garlic, minced
- ○ 2 cups vegetable broth
- ○ 1 head of broccoli, cut into florets
- ○ 1 cup feta cheese, grated (250g)
- ○ ½ cup milk (140ml)
- ○ Salt and pepper, to taste
- ○ ½ tsp thyme (optional)

Method

1. Melt butter in a large pot over medium heat.
2. Add onions, garlic until the onion is soft, about 5 minutes.
3. Stir in vegetable broth, add the thyme, and bring to a simmer.
4. Add the broccoli florets, cover the pot, and simmer for 10 minutes.
5. Remove the pot from the heat and use an immersion blender to blend the soup until smooth.
6. Stir in the cheese and milk and season with salt and pepper.
7. Simmer for an additional 5 minutes, stirring often, until the soup is heated through and the cheese has melted.

Nutrition: 1 serving / whole meal, calories 163 / 653, protein(g) 7 / 28, carbs(g) 5 / 22, fats(g) 13 / 52, fiber(g) 1 / 4, sodium(mg) 483 / 1934, sugar(g) 1 / 7, saturated fat(g) 8 / 32

Creamy Mushroom Soup
4 servings

Prep: 10 min | Cook: 20 min | Total: 30 min

Ingredients

- ○ 1 large onion, diced
- ○ 1 medium head of garlic, minced
- ○ 2 lbs mushrooms, sliced (1kg)
- ○ 2 cups vegetable broth (480ml)
- ○ 1 cup milk (240ml)
- ○ 1 cup feta cheese, grated (250g)
- ○ Salt and pepper, to taste
- ○ 1 tbsp olive oil

Method

1. Heat olive oil in a large pot over medium heat.
2. Add onions and garlic until the onions are soft, about 5 minutes.
3. Add the mushrooms until they are browned and softened, about 10 minutes.
4. Add the vegetable broth and bring to a simmer.
5. Simmer until the mushrooms are tender, about 10 minutes.
6. Remove the pot from the heat and use an immersion blender to blend the soup until smooth.
7. Stir in the milk and cheese and season with salt and pepper.
8. Simmer for an additional 5 minutes, stirring often, until the soup is heated through and the cheese has melted.

Nutrition: 1 serving / whole meal, calories 318 / 1273, protein(g) 17 / 70, carbs(g) 14 / 57, fats(g) 21 / 87, fiber(g) 2 / 11, sodium(mg) 700 / 2801, sugar(g) 5 / 22, saturated fat(g) 10 / 43

Potato Cream Soup
4 servings

Prep: 15 min | Cook: 25 min | Total: 40 min

Method

1. In a large skillet, cook the bacon over medium heat, until browned and crisp for about 10 to 12 minutes. Transfer bacon to paper towels to drain. Once the bacon has cooled, crumble it into small pieces.

2. Warm oil in a large pot over medium heat. Add onion, carrots, and celery. Season with salt and pepper. Stir until vegetables have softened.

3. Add the potatoes and broth. Bring to a boil over high heat; reduce heat to medium-low and simmer.

4. Cook until potatoes are tender.

5. Using an immersion blender, puree soup until smooth.

6. Over medium heat, whisk milk and cream cheese into the soup, stirring constantly until the cream cheese has fully melted. Season with salt and pepper.

7. Divide among 4 bowls, then top with bacon.

Ingredients

- ○ 6 slices bacon, chopped
- ○ 1 medium onion, finely chopped (about 1 cup)
- ○ 1 cup chopped carrots
- ○ 1 cup chopped celery
- ○ 3 regular large potatoes, peeled, cut into 1-inch chunks (about 1 1/2 lbs. / 700 g)
- ○ 3 cups low-sodium chicken broth (750 ml)
- ○ ½ cup milk (120 ml)
- ○ 1 tbsp olive oil
- ○ 4 ounces cream cheese, at room temperature
- ○ Salt and black pepper by taste

Nutrition: 1 serving / whole meal, calories 471 / 1885, protein(g) 17 / 69, carbs(g) 57 / 228, fats(g) 20 / 83, fiber(g) 7 / 29, sodium(mg) 613 / 2453, sugar(g) 3 / 15, saturated fat(g) 9 / 39

Minestrone Soup
4 servings

Prep: 10 min | Cook: 45 min | Total: 55 min

Ingredients

- ◯ 0.8 lbs pasta (400g)
- ◯ 2 tbsp olive oil
- ◯ 1 large onion, diced
- ◯ 2 large carrots, diced
- ◯ 2 stalks celery, diced
- ◯ 3 cloves garlic, minced
- ◯ 1 tsp dried oregano
- ◯ 1 tsp dried thyme
- ◯ 1 tsp dried rosemary
- ◯ 1 (14.5-ounce) can diced tomatoes (400g)
- ◯ 2 small zucchini, diced
- ◯ 1 small head savoy cabbage, chopped
- ◯ 1 (15-ounce) can cannellini beans, drained and rinsed (400g)
- ◯ 4 cups vegetable stock (1000 ml)
- ◯ Salt and pepper to taste

Method

1. Boil the pasta until ready based on the label in a large pot on high heat with a bit of salt.
2. Heat the olive oil in a large pot over medium heat.
3. Add the onion, carrots, celery, garlic, oregano, thyme, and rosemary and cook, stirring occasionally, until the vegetables are softened, about 5 minutes.
4. Add the diced tomatoes, zucchini, cabbage, beans, and vegetable stock and bring to a boil.
5. Drain the cooked pasta and add to the other pot.
6. Reduce the heat to a low simmer, cover, and cook for 30 minutes.
7. Season with salt and pepper to taste.
8. Serve warm.

Nutrition: 1 serving / whole meal, calories 632 / 2530, protein(g) 19 / 79, carbs(g) 103 / 412, fats(g) 15 / 60, fiber(g) 14 / 57, sodium(mg) 667 / 2668, sugar(g) 8 / 33, saturated fat(g) 2 / 10

Mexican Lentil Soup
6 servings

Prep: 15 min | Cook: 45 min | Total: 60 min

Method

1. Heat the olive oil in a large pot over medium heat, then add the onion, garlic until soft, about 5 minutes.

2. Add the carrots, tomato, chili powder and continue to stir for 5 more minutes.

3. Next add the lentils, oregano, smoked paprika, diced tomato, and cumin, stirring to combine.

4. Add the vegetable broth and bring to a boil.

5. Reduce heat to a simmer and simmer for 45 minutes, stirring occasionally.

6. Add the coriander and lime juice and remove from heat.

7. Serve hot.

Ingredients

- ○ 1 tbsp olive oil
- ○ 1 large onion, diced
- ○ 4 cloves garlic, minced
- ○ 2 large carrots, diced
- ○ 1 tsp chili powder (optional)
- ○ 1 large tomato, diced
- ○ 1/2 cup red lentils (100g)
- ○ 1 tsp oregano
- ○ 1/2 tsp smoked paprika
- ○ 1/2 tsp cumin
- ○ 6 cups of vegetable broth (1.5 l)
- ○ 1/4 cup coriander, chopped
- ○ 1/2 lime, juiced

Nutrition: 1 serving / whole meal, calories 186 / 1116, protein(g) 7 / 45, carbs(g) 27 / 162, fats(g) 5 / 33, fiber(g) 8 / 50, sodium(mg) 573 / 3440, sugar(g) 3 / 23, saturated fat(g) 0 / 4

Banana Cupcake

3 servings

Prep: 10 min | Cook: 30 min | Total: 40 min

Ingredients

- ○ 4 medium bananas
- ○ 0.5 lbs nonfat Greek yogurt (250g)
- ○ 3 medium whole eggs
- ○ 1 tbsp baking powder
- ○ 1 tsp vanilla extract

Method

1. In a large bowl, beat the eggs with a fork or whisk until the egg whites and yolks are blended nicely.

2. Peel the bananas and mash them with a fork (or blend them).

3. Inside a separate bowl, pour the yogurt and add the baking powder. Stir them together well.

4. Combine the eggs, bananas, and yogurt in one bowl and mix everything.

5. Pour the mixture into a non-stick cake tin that has baking paper on the bottom and sides.

6. Bake at 350F (180C) for 20-30 minutes until ready. (Wait for a light brown crisp)

7. Split into equal portions and store in the fridge.

Nutrition: 1 serving / whole meal, calories 242 / 728, protein(g) 15 / 46, carbs(g) 34 / 104, fats(g) 4 / 14, fiber(g) 3 / 11, sodium(mg) 300 / 900, sugar(g) 17 / 51, saturated fat(g) 1 / 4

Berry Ice Cream
1 serving

Prep: 5 min | Cook: 5 min | Total: 10 min

Method

1. Clean the blueberries with water if needed.
2. Pour the Greek yogurt, honey, and blueberries into the blender.
3. Blend everything together until the mixture thickens.
4. Split the mixture into equal-sized cups.
5. Put them in the freezer for a minimum of 2-3 hours. (You can optionally leave a few blueberries intact and add them on top for extra flavor and look.)

Ingredients

- ○ 0.5 lbs nonfat Greek yogurt (250g)
- ○ 1 cup of blueberries (150g)
- ○ 1 tbsp of honey

Nutrition: 1 serving / whole meal, calories 286 / 286, protein(g) 23 / 23, carbs(g) 42 / 42, fats(g) 1 / 1, fiber(g) 3 / 3, sodium(mg) 113 / 113, sugar(g) 36 / 36, saturated fat(g) 0 / 0

Chia Pudding
2 servings

Prep: 5 min | Cook: 5 min | Total: 10 min

Ingredients

- ○ 0.5 lbs nonfat Greek yogurt (250g)
- ○ 1 and 3/4 cups of strawberries (250g)
- ○ 1/2 cup of chia seeds (86g)

Method

1. The strawberries are washed nicely, and the leaves are removed. They are left to unfreeze beforehand if frozen.
2. Put all the yogurt and the strawberries in the blender.
3. Blend them until the mixture thickens.
4. Split the mixture into equal-sized cups/dishes and sprinkle the chia seeds evenly.
5. Stir a bit if needed and leave in the fridge for at least 3 hours to cool down.

Nutrition: 1 serving / whole meal, calories 430 / 861, protein(g) 21 / 42, carbs(g) 43 / 87, fats(g) 17 / 35, fiber(g) 30 / 60, sodium(mg) 131 / 262, sugar(g) 14 / 28, saturated fat(g) 1 / 3

Apple Omelette

2 servings

Prep: 10 min | Cook: 20 min | Total: 30 min

Method

1. Wash the apples with hot water, cut them in half and remove the seeds. Grate them and remove all the apple juice by squeezing them with a spoon and a strainer.

2. Put a non-stick pan on a hot plate, add the olive oil, and spread it evenly.

3. Once the olive oil is hot, add the apples and stir until they start to get red. Once ready, remove the pan from the stove.

4. Mix the eggs, cinnamon, and honey in a bowl. Once ready, pour the mixture inside the pan with the apples.

5. Put the pan again on the stove and stir everything well.

6. Cook the omelet and flip it until both sides become golden brown. (around 2 minutes per side)

Ingredients

- ○ 2 large eggs
- ○ 3 medium apples
- ○ 1 tsp cinnamon
- ○ 1 tbsp olive oil
- ○ 1 tbsp honey

Nutrition: 1 serving / whole meal, calories 310 / 621, protein(g) 6 / 12, carbs(g) 30 / 61, fats(g) 20 / 41, fiber(g) 4 / 9, sodium(mg) 64 / 129, sugar(g) 24 / 48, saturated fat(g) 4 / 8

Ingredients

- ○ 2 large eggs
- ○ 3 medium apples
- ○ 2 tbsp honey
- ○ 1 cup almond milk (240ml)
- ○ 1 tbsp baking powder
- ○ 1 tbsp cinnamon
- ○ 1 tsp vanilla extract

Apple Pie
2 servings

Prep: 10 min | Cook: 30 min | Total: 40 min

Method

1. Wash the apples, peel them and remove all the seeds from the middle by cutting them in large pieces.

2. Place the pieces inside a large enough pot and fill it with water and boil for around 10 minutes.

3. Remove the water and wait. Once they are cool enough, grate them using a vegetable grater or any other piece of equipment that would do the job.

4. In a large bowl, mix well the eggs, honey, vanilla, cinnamon, and baking powder until the liquid becomes white. Next, add the milk while stirring. Finally, include the grated apples and mix everything well.

5. Pour the mixture into a non-stick cake tin with some baking paper on the bottom and walls. (Optionally, you can use a bit of olive oil).

6. Bake inside a preheated oven at 350F (180C) until there is a nice brownish crust, until ready. (Use a fork to check if it's done inside)

7. Split into equal portions and meal prep the rest.

Nutrition: 1 serving / whole meal, calories 455 / 911, protein(g) 11 / 23, carbs(g) 74 / 148, fats(g) 14 / 28, fiber(g) 11 / 23, sodium(mg) 339 / 679, sugar(g) 55 / 111, saturated fat(g) 1 / 2

Stuffed Pears w/ Honey

3 servings

Prep: 10 min | Cook: 30 min | Total: 40 min

Ingredients

- ○ 5 medium ripe pears
- ○ 2 tbsp cinnamon
- ○ 3 tbsp honey
- ○ 1 walnut

Method

1. Wash the pears nicely with hot water.
2. Cut them in half (on their long side) and remove all the seeds.
3. Use a spoon (or anything else) to carve them close to the walls without going through them. Collect the insides in a separate bowl.
4. Once ready, blend the pear insides with the honey and cinnamon until everything is nicely mixed.
5. Line up the pears inside a large enough tray with baking paper on the bottom.
6. Once lined, fill them with the blended mixture evenly and bake them in a preheated oven/air fryer at 350F (180C) until ready.
7. Optionally, you can sprinkle 1 crushed walnut on top once they are done for extra flavor.

Nutrition: 1 serving / whole meal, calories 218 / 655, protein(g) 1 / 4, carbs(g) 56 / 169, fats(g) 0 / 1, fiber(g) 10 / 31, sodium(mg) 2 / 6, sugar(g) 44 / 133, saturated fat(g) 0 / 0

Carrot Cake Oatmeal

4 servings

Prep: 10 min | Cook: 10 min | Total: 20 min

Method

1. Combine the oats, carrot, walnuts, cinnamon, and nutmeg in a bowl.

2. In a separate bowl, whisk together the vanilla, honey, and almond milk.

3. Pour the wet ingredients into the dry ingredients and mix until everything is combined.

4. Divide the mixture among four oven-safe ramekins and bake in a 350°F oven for 10 minutes.

Ingredients

- ○ 1 ½ cup rolled oats (120g)
- ○ 1 cup grated carrot
- ○ ¼ cup chopped walnuts
- ○ 1 tsp ground cinnamon
- ○ ¼ tsp ground nutmeg
- ○ 1 tsp vanilla extract
- ○ 2 tsp honey
- ○ 1 cup almond milk

Nutrition: 1 serving / whole meal, calories 234 / 936, protein(g) 6 / 27, carbs(g) 38 / 152, fats(g) 7 / 29, fiber(g) 6 / 25, sodium(mg) 69 / 277, sugar(g) 10 / 43, saturated fat(g) 0 / 2

Banana Coconut Cake
8 servings

Prep: 10 min | Cook: 15 min | Total: 25 min

Method

1. Mash the bananas in a bowl with a fork.
2. Whisk the eggs, coconut oil, and almond milk together in a separate bowl.
3. In a third bowl, combine the oat flour, baking powder, and sea salt.
4. Add the wet ingredients to the dry ingredients and mix until combined.
5. Fold in the mashed bananas and shredded coconut.
6. Pour the mixture into an 8-inch cake pan and bake in a 350°F oven for 15 minutes.

Ingredients

- ○ 2 large ripe bananas
- ○ 2 medium eggs
- ○ 2 tbsp coconut oil
- ○ 1 cup almond milk
- ○ 1 cup oat flour
- ○ 1 tsp baking powder
- ○ Pinch of sea salt
- ○ ¼ cup shredded coconut (18g)

Nutrition: 1 serving / whole meal, calories 145 / 1166, protein(g) 4 / 32, carbs(g) 15 / 123, fats(g) 8 / 68, fiber(g) 3 / 24, sodium(mg) 53 / 424, sugar(g) 4 / 36, saturated fat(g) 2 / 22

Avocado Cheesecake
8 servings

Prep: 15 min | Cook: 1 h 0 min | Total: 1 h 15 min

Ingredients

- ○ 1 ½ cups graham cracker crumbs (180g)
- ○ 1 ½ tsp sugar (for crust)
- ○ 3 tbsp melted butter
- ○ 2 large eggs
- ○ 2 medium avocados
- ○ 2/3 cup low-fat Greek yogurt
- ○ 1/3 cup fat-free cream cheese
- ○ 3 tbsp cornstarch
- ○ 1 tsp vanilla extract
- ○ 1/3 cup sugar (for filling)

Method

1. Mix the graham cracker crumbs and the sugar in a bowl.
2. Add the melted butter and mix until all the crumbs are evenly moistened.
3. Press the mixture evenly into a 9-inch springform pan.
4. Bake at 350°F (180 C) for 8-10 minutes.
5. In a separate bowl, mash the avocados and then add the Greek yogurt, cream cheese, cornstarch, vanilla extract, eggs and the 1/3 cup of sugar.
6. Mix until smooth.
7. Carefully pour the filling over the crust.
8. Bake at 350°F (180 C) for 50-55 minutes.
9. Cool in the refrigerator overnight.

Nutrition: 1 serving / whole meal, calories 285 / 2285, protein(g) 9 / 74, carbs(g) 29 / 235, fats(g) 16 / 132, fiber(g) 3 / 25, sodium(mg) 183 / 1469, sugar(g) 16 / 133, saturated fat(g) 7 / 62

Greek Yogurt Cheesecake
8 servings

Prep: 10 min | Cook: 1 h 15 min | Total: 1 h 25 min

Ingredients

- ○ 1 ½ cups graham cracker crumbs (180g)
- ○ 2 tbsp sugar (for crust)
- ○ 5 tbsp melted butter
- ○ 2 large eggs
- ○ 1 cup low-fat Greek yogurt
- ○ 1 cup fat-free cream cheese
- ○ 3 tbsp cornstarch
- ○ 1 tsp vanilla extract
- ○ 1/3 cup sugar (for filling)

Method

1. Mix the graham cracker crumbs and 2 tbsp sugar in a bowl.
2. Add the melted butter and mix until all the crumbs are evenly moistened.
3. Press the mixture into the bottom of a 9-inch springform pan.
4. Bake at 350°F (180 C) for 8-10 minutes.
5. In a separate bowl, beat the eggs and add the Greek yogurt, cream cheese, cornstarch, vanilla extract, and 1/3 cup of sugar.
6. Mix until smooth.
7. Carefully pour the filling over the crust.
8. Bake at 350°F for 55-60 minutes.
9. Cool in the refrigerator overnight.

Nutrition: 1 serving / whole meal, calories 244 / 1957, protein(g) 9 / 77, carbs(g) 22 / 178, fats(g) 13 / 111, fiber(g) 0 / 2, sodium(mg) 212 / 1701, sugar(g) 10 / 85, saturated fat(g) 7 / 62

Apple Smoothie

1 serving

Prep: 5 min | Cook: 1 min | Total: 6 min

Ingredients

- ○ 1 medium apple
- ○ 1 medium kiwi
- ○ 1 cup of milk by choice (low fat, almond or coconut) (240ml)
- ○ 1 tbsp honey
- ○ 1 cup/a handful of blueberries (150g)
- ○ 3-4 ice cubes (optional)

Method

1. Place inside a blender the sliced apple (no seeds, peel optional), milk, sliced kiwi (peeled), honey and blueberries.

2. Blend until the liquid becomes thick (approx 1 min.)

3. Pour the smoothie into a cup and drink. (best suited for first thing in the morning).

4. Store in the fridge if you are not going to drink it immediately. Drink within 24-48 hours.

Nutrition: 1 serving / whole meal, calories 304 / 304, protein(g) 9 / 9, carbs(g) 60 / 60, fats(g) 5 / 5, fiber(g) 6 / 6, sodium(mg) 100 / 100, sugar(g) 44 / 44, saturated fat(g) 3 / 3

Pumpkin Smoothie
1 serving

Prep: 5 min | Cook: 5 min | Total: 10 min

Method

1. The simplest way to cook the pumpkin is to cut it in peel it, cut it in small pieces, remove the seeds and boil it on medium heat until soft and ready. (or buy cooked instead)

2. Cut the pumpkin and the banana into about 2-inch pieces (5 cm) so they can fit inside the blender.

3. Add them inside the blender with the milk, cinnamon, and honey.

4. Blend the mixture until the liquid becomes thick.

5. Pour into a cup and drink.

Ingredients

- ○ 1 medium banana
- ○ 1 cup almond milk (240ml)
- ○ 0.2 lbs cooked pumpkin (100g)
- ○ 1 tbsp cinnamon
- ○ 1 tbsp honey

Nutrition: 1 serving / whole meal, calories 207 / 207, protein(g) 4 / 4, carbs(g) 45 / 45, fats(g) 3 / 3, fiber(g) 7 / 7, sodium(mg) 203 / 203, sugar(g) 23 / 23, saturated fat(g) 0 / 0

Coffee Smoothie

1 serving

Prep: 10 min | Cook: 5 min | Total: 15 min

Method

1. Prepare a normal cup of coffee with boiling water and 1 tbsp of black pure coffee. (or use a coffee machine).

2. Once the coffee is cooled down a bit, pour it inside a blender, add the peeled banana crushed in 2/3 similar pieces, and add the cinnamon. You can optionally add a few cubes of ice.

3. Blend until the liquid becomes thick.

4. Pour the smoothie into a cup and drink. (best suited for first thing in the morning).

Ingredients

- ○ 1 medium banana
- ○ 1 cup of coffee (pure black) (240 ml)
- ○ 1 tsp of cinnamon
- ○ 3-4 ice cubes (optional)

Nutrition: 1 serving / whole meal, calories 106 / 106, protein(g) 1 / 1, carbs(g) 26 / 26, fats(g) 0 / 0, fiber(g) 3 / 3, sodium(mg) 1 / 1, sugar(g) 12 / 12, saturated fat(g) 0 / 0

Banana Smoothie

1 serving

Prep: 5 min | Cook: 1 min | Total: 6 min

Ingredients

- ○ 1 medium banana
- ○ 1 tbsp honey
- ○ 1 cup milk of your choice (low fat, almond or coconut) (240ml)
- ○ 1 tsp of cinnamon
- ○ 3-4 ice cubes (optional)

Method

1. Place inside a blender the sliced banana, milk, honey, and cinnamon.
2. Blend until the liquid becomes thick (approx 1 min.)
3. Pour the smoothie into a cup and drink. (best suited for first thing in the morning).
4. Leave in the fridge if you are not going to drink immediately. Drink within 24-48 hours.

Nutrition: 1 serving / whole meal, calories 236 / 236, protein(g) 7 / 7, carbs(g) 43 / 43, fats(g) 5 / 5, fiber(g) 2 / 2, sodium(mg) 95 / 95, sugar(g) 33 / 33, saturated fat(g) 3 / 3

Avocado Smoothie

1 serving

Prep: 5 min | Cook: 1 min | Total: 6 min

Method

1. Place inside a blender the sliced avocado (medium pieces), milk, sliced banana (peeled), and the coconut oil.
2. Blend until the liquid becomes thick (approx 1 min.)
3. Pour the smoothie into a cup and drink. (best suited for first thing in the morning).
4. Leave in fridge if you are not going to drink immediately.
5. Drink within 24-48 hours.

Ingredients

- ○ 1/2 medium avocado
- ○ 1 medium banana
- ○ 1 cup of milk by choice (low fat, almond or coconut) (240ml)
- ○ 1 tsp coconut oil
- ○ 3-4 ice cubes (optional)

Nutrition: 1 serving / whole meal, calories 348 / 348, protein(g) 9 / 9, carbs(g) 31 / 31, fats(g) 23 / 23, fiber(g) 9 / 9, sodium(mg) 107 / 107, sugar(g) 12 / 12, saturated fat(g) 6 / 6

Mango Smoothie
1 serving

Prep: 5 min | Cook: 1 min | Total: 6 min

Method

1. Peel and cut into small pieces the mango and place it inside the blender
2. Peel and cut into medium pieces the banana (remove the ends) and place them inside the blender.
3. Pour the milk and put the lid on.
4. Blend until the liquid becomes thick (approx 30 sec - 1 min)
5. Pour the smoothie into a cup and drink. (best suited for first thing in the morning).
6. Leave in the fridge if you are not going to drink it immediately.
7. Drink within 24-48 hours.

Ingredients

- ○ 1 medium mango
- ○ 1 medium banana
- ○ 1 cup of milk by choice (low fat, almond or coconut) (240 ml)
- ○ 3-4 ice cubes (optional)

Nutrition: 1 serving / whole meal, calories 288 / 288, protein(g) 7 / 7, carbs(g) 58 / 58, fats(g) 3 / 3, fiber(g) 6 / 6, sodium(mg) 114 / 114, sugar(g) 38 / 38, saturated fat(g) 2 / 2

Tropical Fruit Protein Smoothie
2 servings

Prep: 10 min | Cook: 0 min | Total: 10 min

Method

1. Add all ingredients to a blender and blend until smooth.
2. Serve and enjoy!

Ingredients

- ○ 1/4 cup mango, frozen
- ○ 1/4 cup pineapple, frozen
- ○ 1 banana, peeled and frozen
- ○ 1/2 cup plain Greek yogurt
- ○ 1/4 cup almond milk
- ○ 1 scoop vanilla protein powder
- ○ 1 tsp honey (optional)

Nutrition: 1 serving / whole meal, calories 189 / 379, protein(g) 14 / 29, carbs(g) 26 / 53, fats(g) 2 / 5, fiber(g) 3 / 7, sodium(mg) 92 / 184, sugar(g) 17 / 34, saturated fat(g) 0 / 1

Green Smoothie
1 serving

Prep: 5 min | Cook: 0 min | Total: 5 min

Method

1. Add all ingredients to a blender and blend until smooth.
2. Serve and enjoy!

Ingredients

- ○ 1 banana, peeled and frozen
- ○ 1 cup spinach, frozen
- ○ 1/2 cup pineapple, frozen
- ○ 1/2 cup mango, frozen
- ○ 1/2 cup plain Greek yogurt
- ○ 1/2 cup almond milk
- ○ 1 tsp chia seeds
- ○ 1/2 tsp ginger, freshly grated
- ○ 1/2 tsp turmeric

Nutrition: 1 serving / whole meal, calories 343 / 343, protein(g) 22 / 22, carbs(g) 58 / 58, fats(g) 5 / 5, fiber(g) 12 / 12, sodium(mg) 180 / 180, sugar(g) 36 / 36, saturated fat(g) 1 / 1

Pineapple Smoothie
1 serving

Prep: 5 min | Cook: 0 min | Total: 5 min

Method

1. Add all the ingredients to a blender.
2. Blend until smooth and creamy.
3. Pour into a glass and enjoy.

Ingredients

- ○ 1 cup pineapple cubes
- ○ 1 banana
- ○ 1/2 cup plain Greek yogurt (120g)
- ○ 1/2 cup milk (120ml)
- ○ 1/2 cup ice cubes
- ○ 1 tsp honey

Nutrition: 1 serving / whole meal, calories 253 / 253, protein(g) 15 / 15, carbs(g) 41 / 41, fats(g) 4 / 4, fiber(g) 3 / 3, sodium(mg) 106 / 106, sugar(g) 30 / 30, saturated fat(g) 2 / 2

Pineapple, Mango Smoothie
1 serving

Prep: 5 min | Cook: 0 min | Total: 5 min

Method

1. Add all the ingredients to a blender.
2. Blend until smooth and creamy.
3. Pour into a glass and enjoy.

Ingredients

- ◯ 1/2 cup pineapple cubes (75g)
- ◯ 1/2 cup mango cubes (75g)
- ◯ 1/2 cup plain Greek yogurt (120g)
- ◯ 1/2 cup almond milk (120 ml)
- ◯ 1/2 cup ice cubes (60g)
- ◯ 1 tsp honey

Nutrition: 1 serving / whole meal, calories 198 / 198, protein(g) 12 / 12, carbs(g) 28 / 28, fats(g) 5 / 5, fiber(g) 2 / 2, sodium(mg) 115 / 115, sugar(g) 23 / 23, saturated fat(g) 1 / 1

Strawberry Banana Smoothie

1 serving

Prep: 5 min | Cook: 0 min | Total: 5 min

Method

1. Add all ingredients to a blender.
2. Blend until smooth and creamy.
3. Pour into glasses and serve immediately.

Ingredients

- ○ 2 ripe bananas
- ○ 1 cup fresh strawberries
- ○ 1 cup unsweetened almond milk (240ml)
- ○ 1/2 cup plain Greek yogurt (120g)
- ○ 1 tbsp honey
- ○ 1/2 tsp vanilla extract
- ○ 1 cup ice cubes

Nutrition: 1 serving / whole meal, calories 385 / 385, protein(g) 17 / 17, carbs(g) 76 / 76, fats(g) 5 / 5, fiber(g) 9 / 9, sodium(mg) 181 / 181, sugar(g) 51 / 51, saturated fat(g) 1 / 1

Orange Creamsicle Smoothie
1 serving

Prep: 5 min | Cook: 0 min | Total: 5 min

Method

1. Add all ingredients to a blender and blend until smooth.
2. Serve immediately and enjoy!

Ingredients

- ○ 1 medium orange, peeled and seeded
- ○ 1/2 medium banana, peeled
- ○ 1/2 cup unsweetened almond milk
- ○ 1/4 cup plain Greek yogurt
- ○ 1/2 tsp vanilla extract
- ○ 1 tbsp honey
- ○ 1/2 cup ice cubes

Nutrition: 1 serving / whole meal, calories 203 / 203, protein(g) 7 / 7, carbs(g) 42 / 42, fats(g) 3 / 3, fiber(g) 3 / 3, sodium(mg) 108 / 108, sugar(g) 32 / 32, saturated fat(g) 0 / 0

Green Apple Smoothie

1 serving

Prep: 5 min | Cook: 0 min | Total: 5 min

Ingredients

- ○ 1 medium-sized green apple, chopped
- ○ 1 cup spinach
- ○ 1/2 cup unsweetened almond milk
- ○ 1/2 cup water
- ○ 1/2 banana
- ○ 1/2 tsp ground cinnamon
- ○ 1/2 tsp vanilla extract
- ○ 1 tsp honey (optional)
- ○ Ice cubes (optional)

Method

1. Add the chopped green apple and spinach to a blender.
2. Pour in the almond milk and water.
3. Add the banana, ground cinnamon, and vanilla extract.
4. Optionally, add honey for sweetness and ice cubes for a colder smoothie.
5. Blend all the ingredients until smooth and creamy.
6. Pour the smoothie into a glass and serve immediately. Enjoy!

Nutrition: 1 serving / whole meal, calories 107 / 107, protein(g) 2 / 2, carbs(g) 27 / 27, fats(g) 1 / 1, fiber(g) 5 / 5, sodium(mg) 107 / 107, sugar(g) 17 / 17, saturated fat(g) 0 / 0

Banana Berry Smoothie
1 serving

Prep: 5 min | Cook: 0 min | Total: 5 min

Method

1. Add all ingredients to a blender and blend until smooth.
2. Pour into a glass and enjoy.

Ingredients

- ○ 1 ripe banana
- ○ 1/2 cup frozen mixed berries (100g)
- ○ 1/2 cup almond milk (120ml)
- ○ 1/2 cup ice

Nutrition: 1 serving / whole meal, calories 142 / 142, protein(g) 2 / 2, carbs(g) 34 / 34, fats(g) 2 / 2, fiber(g) 5 / 5, sodium(mg) 94 / 94, sugar(g) 20 / 20, saturated fat(g) 0 / 0

Tropical Green Smoothie
1 serving

Prep: 5 min | Cook: 0 min | Total: 5 min

Method

1. Place all ingredients in a blender and blend until smooth.
2. Pour into a glass and enjoy!

Ingredients

- ○ 1 cup frozen pineapple chunks (140g)
- ○ 1 small ripe banana
- ○ 1 cup packed baby spinach leaves (30g)
- ○ 1/2 cup unsweetened coconut milk (120ml)
- ○ 1/2 cup cold water (12 ml)
- ○ 1/2 tbsp honey

Nutrition: 1 serving / whole meal, calories 177 / 177, protein(g) 2 / 2, carbs(g) 43 / 43, fats(g) 3 / 3, fiber(g) 4 / 4, sodium(mg) 85 / 85, sugar(g) 28 / 28, saturated fat(g) 2 / 2

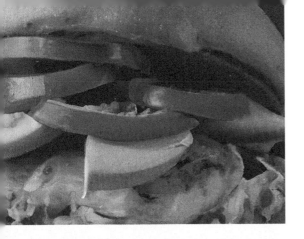

Chicken Avocado Burger
2 servings

Prep: 15 min | Cook: 15 min | Total: 30 min

Method

1. Preheat the grill to medium-high heat.
2. In a large bowl, combine ground chicken, breadcrumbs, egg, garlic powder, onion powder, salt, and pepper. Mix well.
3. Divide the chicken mixture into 2 equal parts and shape into burger patties.
4. Grill the chicken burgers for about 5-6 minutes on each side, or until they are fully cooked.
5. Meanwhile, toast the buns on the grill.
6. Once the chicken burgers are done, assemble the burgers by placing lettuce leaves on the bottom bun, followed by a slice of tomato, a slice of red onion, the chicken burger, and slices of avocado. Cover with the top bun and serve immediately.

Ingredients

- ○ 1 lb ground chicken (500g)
- ○ 1/4 cup breadcrumbs
- ○ 1 medium egg
- ○ 1/2 tsp garlic powder
- ○ 1/2 tsp onion powder
- ○ Salt and black pepper (by taste)
- ○ 2 whole wheat buns
- ○ 1 avocado, sliced
- ○ 1 medium tomato, sliced
- ○ 4 lettuce leaves
- ○ 4 slices of red onion

Nutrition: 1 serving / whole meal, calories 436 / 872, protein(g) 29 / 58, carbs(g) 31 / 62, fats(g) 21 / 43, fiber(g) 10 / 20, sodium(mg) 278 / 557, sugar(g) 4 / 8, saturated fat(g) 4 / 8

Portobello Mushroom Burger
4 servings

Prep: 10 min | Cook: 20 min | Total: 30 min

Ingredients

- ◯ 4 portobello mushroom caps
- ◯ 1/4 cup balsamic vinegar
- ◯ 1 tbsp olive oil
- ◯ 1 tsp garlic powder
- ◯ 1 tsp onion powder
- ◯ 1 tsp smoked paprika
- ◯ 4 whole wheat burger buns
- ◯ 1 ripe avocado, sliced
- ◯ 1/2 red onion, sliced
- ◯ 1 small tomato, sliced
- ◯ Salt and pepper to taste
- ◯ Optional toppings: mustard, ketchup, hot sauce

Method

1. Preheat the oven to 400°F (200°C).
2. Clean the portobello mushroom caps with a damp paper towel and remove the stems.
3. In a small bowl, whisk together the balsamic vinegar, olive oil, garlic powder, onion powder, and smoked paprika.
4. Place the mushroom caps in a baking dish and brush both sides with the marinade.
5. Bake for 10-15 minutes or until the mushrooms are tender and juicy.
6. Meanwhile, toast the burger buns and prepare the toppings.
7. Assemble the burgers by placing a mushroom cap on each bun, followed by the avocado slices, red onion slices, tomato slices, and any other desired toppings.
8. Season with salt and pepper to taste.
9. Serve immediately and enjoy!

Nutrition: 1 serving / whole meal, calories 263 / 1052, protein(g) 6 / 26, carbs(g) 43 / 172, fats(g) 8 / 32, fiber(g) 9 / 38, sodium(mg) 212 / 851, sugar(g) 4 / 19, saturated fat(g) 1 / 5

Grilled Chicken Burger
4 servings

Prep: 20 min | Cook: 10 min | Total: 30 min

Method

1. Preheat a grill or grill pan over medium-high heat.
2. In a bowl, combine the ground chicken, grated onion, minced garlic, chopped parsley, dried oregano, and a pinch of salt and pepper.
3. Mix well and shape the mixture into 4 patties.
4. Grill the patties for 4-5 minutes on each side, or until they're cooked through.
5. While the patties are cooking, toast the burger buns until lightly browned.
6. Assemble the burgers by placing a lettuce leaf, a slice of tomato, a slice of red onion, and some sliced cucumber on the bottom half of each burger bun. Place a chicken patty on top, and cover with the top half of the bun.
7. Serve immediately.

Ingredients

- ○ 1 lb ground chicken (500 g)
- ○ 1 small onion, grated
- ○ 1 garlic clove, minced
- ○ 2 tbsp fresh parsley, chopped
- ○ 1 tsp dried oregano
- ○ Salt and pepper (by taste)
- ○ 4 whole wheat burger buns
- ○ 4 lettuce leaves
- ○ 4 slices of tomato
- ○ 4 slices of red onion
- ○ 1 small cucumber, sliced

Nutrition: 1 serving / whole meal, calories 310 / 1240, protein(g) 29 / 116, carbs(g) 28 / 114, fats(g) 9 / 36, fiber(g) 4 / 17, sodium(mg) 167 / 670, sugar(g) 2 / 10, saturated fat(g) 1 / 6

Sweet Potato & Veggie Burgers
4 servings

Prep: 15 min | Cook: 15 min | Total: 30 min

Ingredients

- ○ 1 large sweet potato, peeled and grated
- ○ 1 (15 oz) can of chickpeas, drained and rinsed (400g)
- ○ 1/2 cup breadcrumbs
- ○ 1/4 cup cilantro, chopped
- ○ 1/4 cup parsley, chopped
- ○ 2 tbsp olive oil
- ○ 1 tsp garlic powder
- ○ 1/4 tsp sea salt
- ○ 1/4 tsp black pepper
- ○ 1 avocado, mashed
- ○ 4 whole wheat buns

Method

1. In a large bowl, mix the grated sweet potato, chickpeas, breadcrumbs, cilantro, parsley, olive oil, garlic powder, salt, and pepper.

2. Shape the mixture into four burger patties.

3. Heat a skillet over medium heat and cook the patties for 7 minutes per side, or until golden and crispy.

4. Assemble the burgers with a layer of mashed avocado and serve with a whole wheat bun. Inside the buns, you can add whatever you like.

5. Enjoy!

Nutrition: 1 serving / whole meal, calories 330 / 1320, protein(g) 8 / 33, carbs(g) 56 / 226, fats(g) 9 / 36, fiber(g) 9 / 38, sodium(mg) 247 / 990, sugar(g) 2 / 10, saturated fat(g) 1 / 5

Homemade BBQ Pork Burgers
4 servings

Prep: 10 min | Cook: 10 min | Total: 20 min

Ingredients

- ○ 1 lb ground pork (500g)
- ○ 1 small sweet onion, minced (50g)
- ○ 2 cloves garlic, minced
- ○ 2 tbsp BBQ sauce (30 ml)
- ○ 2 tsp Worcestershire sauce (10 ml)
- ○ 1 tsp brown sugar
- ○ 1 tsp garlic powder
- ○ 1 tsp smoked paprika
- ○ 1 tsp chili powder (optional)
- ○ Salt and black pepper to taste
- ○ Lettuce leaves (optional)
- ○ Slices of tomato (optional)
- ○ Slices of pickles (optional)

Method

1. In a large bowl, combine pork, onion, garlic, BBQ sauce, Worcestershire sauce, brown sugar, garlic powder, smoked paprika, chili powder, salt, and pepper. Mix until all ingredients are evenly distributed.

2. Form the mixture into 4 patties.

3. Heat a large skillet over medium heat. Add the patties and cook for about 5 minutes per side, or until cooked through.

4. Slice the buns in half and serve the burgers with your favorite toppings like tomato slices, lettuce leaves, and a bit of BBQ sauce.

Nutrition: 1 serving / whole meal, calories 320 / 1280, protein(g) 26 / 104, carbs(g) 5 / 22, fats(g) 22 / 88, fiber(g) 0 / 2, sodium(mg) 132 / 530, sugar(g) 2 / 9, saturated fat(g) 7 / 29

Mediterranean Pork Burgers
4 servings

Prep: 10 min | Cook: 10 min | Total: 20 min

Ingredients

- ○ 1 lb ground pork (500g)
- ○ ½ cup diced onion (50g)
- ○ ½ cup crumbled feta cheese (50g)
- ○ ¼ cup chopped fresh parsley
- ○ ¼ cup chopped fresh oregano
- ○ 2 cloves garlic, minced
- ○ 2 tbsp olive oil
- ○ 1 tbsp lemon juice
- ○ 1 tsp ground cumin
- ○ Salt and black pepper to taste
- ○ 4 whole wheat buns
- ○ 1 tomato (slices)
- ○ A few lettuce leaves
- ○ Salt and black pepper to taste

Method

1. In a large bowl, combine pork, onion, feta, parsley, oregano, garlic, olive oil, lemon juice, cumin, salt, and pepper.

2. Mix until all ingredients are evenly distributed.

3. Form the mixture into 4 patties.

4. Heat a large skillet over medium heat.

5. Add the patties and cook for about 5 minutes per side, or until cooked through.

6. Slice the buns in half and serve the burgers with your favorite toppings like tomato slices, lettuce leaves, and a bit of BBQ sauce.

Nutrition: 1 serving / whole meal, calories 405 / 1620, protein(g) 24 / 96, carbs(g) 17 / 69, fats(g) 27 / 111, fiber(g) 2 / 8, sodium(mg) 277 / 1110, sugar(g) 1 / 6, saturated fat(g) 8 / 32

Homemade Simple Burgers
2 servings

Prep: 10 min | Cook: 15 min | Total: 25 min

Ingredients

- ○ 1 lb pork mince (500 g)
- ○ 2 burger buns
- ○ 2 slices of feta cheese
- ○ 1 medium head red onion
- ○ 2 pickles (sliced)
- ○ 1 tsp BBQ Sauce
- ○ Salt by taste

Method

1. Slice the buns in half, peel and chop the onion in medium pieces and chop the pickles in circles.
2. Preheat the BBQ grill or grill pan to 350 F (180 C)
3. Separate the meat into 2 equal sizes and form 2 burgers. (You can add different spices for flavor.)
4. Grill the burgers on each side until they are ready. Before they are ready add the onion and buns for a couple of minutes next to them.
5. Once everything is ready combine all the ingredients as you like.
6. Enjoy!

Nutrition: 1 serving / whole meal, calories 640 / 1280, protein(g) 44 / 88, carbs(g) 37 / 74, fats(g) 35 / 70, fiber(g) 3 / 6, sodium(mg) 555 / 1110, sugar(g) 6 / 12, saturated fat(g) 15 / 30

Homemade Tilapia Burgers

4 servings

Prep: 20 min | Cook: 20 min | Total: 40 min

Method

1. Place tilapia in the bowl of a food processor and pulse until finely chopped.
2. Heat 1 tablespoon olive oil in a skillet over medium-high heat.
3. Add white parts of the green onions, bell pepper, celery, and garlic to the hot oil and saute until they start to brown (5-7 minutes).
4. Add green parts of the green onions and parsley; saute for 2-3 minutes more. Let it cool down for 10 minutes.
5. Combine the veggie mixture with the fish. Add salt, onion powder, garlic powder, red pepper flakes, and black pepper; mix with your hands until well combined.
6. Mix in bread crumbs and egg until thoroughly combined.
7. Shape into burger-sized patties.
8. Heat the remaining olive oil on a griddle over medium to medium-high heat. Cook the patties in the hot oil, working in batches as needed, until nicely browned, 3 to 5 minutes on each side.
9. Slice the buns in half and decorate with a slice of tomato, lettuce, and a bit of BBQ sauce.

Ingredients

- ○ 4 burger buns (sliced in half)
- ○ 1 large tomato (cut in thin slices)
- ○ A couple of lettuce leaves & BBQ sauce (optional)
- ○ 5 (4 ounces) filets tilapia (cut into cubes)
- ○ 2-3 tbsp olive oil
- ○ 2 bunches green onions, thinly sliced (green tops separated from white bottoms)
- ○ 1 medium bell pepper (minced)
- ○ 2 stalks celery (minced)
- ○ 4 cloves garlic (chopped)
- ○ 1 pinch onion, garlic powder, red pepper flakes and chopped parsley
- ○ 1 cup panko bread crumbs
- ○ 1 large egg
- ○ Salt and black pepper by taste

Nutrition: 1 serving / whole meal, calories 467 / 1870, protein(g) 29 / 116, carbs(g) 52 / 208, fats(g) 16 / 67, fiber(g) 4 / 18, sodium(mg) 337 / 1350, sugar(g) 4 / 18, saturated fat(g) 2 / 10

Salmon & Zucchini Burgers

4 servings

Prep: 30 min | Cook: 10 min | Total: 40 min

Ingredients

- ○ 4 salmon filets (4 oz/113 g each)
- ○ 1 large zucchini, grated
- ○ 1 tbsp olive oil
- ○ 1 tsp garlic powder, onion powder and paprika
- ○ ½ tsp cumin
- ○ Salt and black pepper by taste
- ○ 1 pinch chili powder (optional)
- ○ 2 tbsp fresh parsley
- ○ 2 tbsp fresh cilantro
- ○ 1 large egg
- ○ 1 cup breadcrumbs (90g)
- ○ 4 burger buns (sliced in half)
- ○ 1 large tomato (cut in thin slices)
- ○ A couple lettuce leaves
- ○ 1 tbsp BBQ sauce (optional)

Method

1. Lightly beat the egg in a large mixing bowl. Add the salmon filets, breaking apart any large chunks gently with your fingers as you add it. (you can blend them optionally)

2. If your zucchini is very wet, squeeze out the excess moisture in a paper towel.

3. Add the zucchini, scallions, crumbs, and all the spices to the bowl and mix gently but thoroughly.

4. Form into 4 round patties. Set on a plate, cover well, and refrigerate until you are ready to cook.

5. Place the patties on a preheated griddle and cook for 5 minutes on each side with the olive oil.

6. Once ready, create 6 burgers with each patty, add tomato slices, lettuce leaves, and a bit of BBQ sauce.

7. Enjoy!

Nutrition: 1 serving / whole meal, calories 485 / 1940, protein(g) 26 / 104, carbs(g) 49 / 197, fats(g) 19 / 79, fiber(g) 4 / 18, sodium(mg) 360 / 1440, sugar(g) 3 / 12, saturated fat(g) 3 / 14

Grilled Salmon Burgers

4 servings

Prep: 10 min | Cook: 10 min | Total: 20 min

Ingredients

- ○ 1 lb wild-caught salmon (500g)
- ○ 2 large eggs
- ○ 2 tbsp finely grated onion
- ○ 2 tsp prepared horseradish (optional)
- ○ 2 tsp fresh lemon juice
- ○ 1/4 cup fresh breadcrumbs
- ○ 1/4 tsp garlic powder
- ○ 1/4 tsp smoked paprika
- ○ 1/4 tsp pepper
- ○ 2-3 tbsp olive oil
- ○ 4 burger buns (sliced in half)
- ○ 1 large tomato (cut in thin slices)
- ○ A couple of lettuce leaves
- ○ 2 pickles (optional)
- ○ 1 tbsp BBQ sauce (optional)

Method

1. Mash the salmon with a fork in a large bowl until it is broken down into small pieces.
2. Add the eggs, onion, horseradish, lemon juice, bread crumbs, garlic powder, smoked paprika, and pepper.
3. Mix until all ingredients are combined.
4. Form into 4 equal patties.
5. Heat the olive oil in a large skillet over medium heat.
6. Place the burgers in the skillet and cook for 4-5 minutes per side or until the burgers are cooked through.
7. Serve the burgers on their own or with a bun with all the extras such as pickles, tomato slices, lettuce leaves, BBQ sauce, etc.

Nutrition: 1 serving / whole meal, calories 407 / 1630, protein(g) 26 / 106, carbs(g) 30 / 123, fats(g) 19 / 79, fiber(g) 2 / 8, sodium(mg) 257 / 1030, sugar(g) 2 / 9, saturated fat(g) 3 / 14

Whole Wheat Veggie Pizza
4 servings

Prep: 15 min | Cook: 15 min | Total: 30 min

Ingredients

- ○ 1 cup whole wheat flour (120g)
- ○ 1 tsp active dry yeast
- ○ 3/4 cup warm water (180ml)
- ○ 1 tsp honey
- ○ 2 tbsp olive oil
- ○ 1/2 tsp garlic powder
- ○ 1/2 tsp salt
- ○ 1/4 cup marina sauce (60ml)
- ○ 1/2 cup low-fat mozzarella cheese (60g)
- ○ 1 large tomato, diced
- ○ 1/4 cup red onion, diced
- ○ 1/4 cup bell pepper, diced
- ○ 1/4 cup mushrooms, diced
- ○ 1/4 tsp black pepper
- ○ 1/4 tsp oregano

Method

1. In a medium bowl, combine the whole wheat flour, active dry yeast, honey, garlic powder, and salt.
2. Add the warm water and olive oil, and mix until all the ingredients are combined.
3. Knead the dough for 2-3 minutes, then cover the bowl with a kitchen towel and let it sit for 10 minutes.
4. Preheat the oven to 425°F (218°C).
5. On a lightly floured work surface, roll out the pizza dough.
6. Transfer the pizza dough to a baking sheet.
7. Spread the marina sauce on the pizza dough.
8. Top it with the mozzarella cheese, tomato, red onion, bell pepper, and mushrooms.
9. Sprinkle the black pepper and oregano on top.
10. Bake for 15 minutes.

Nutrition: 1 serving / whole meal, calories 193 / 774, protein(g) 8 / 33, carbs(g) 25 / 102, fats(g) 6 / 26, fiber(g) 4 / 17, sodium(mg) 199 / 798, sugar(g) 1 / 7, saturated fat(g) 1 / 6

Pesto and Spinach Pizza
4 servings

Prep: 15 min | Cook: 15 min | Total: 30 min

Ingredients

- ○ 1 cup whole wheat flour (120g)
- ○ 1 tsp active dry yeast
- ○ 3/4 cup warm water (180ml)
- ○ 2 tbsp olive oil
- ○ 1 tsp garlic powder
- ○ 1/2 tsp salt
- ○ 2 cups spinach (60g)
- ○ 1/4 cup pesto (60ml)
- ○ 1/2 cup low-fat mozzarella cheese (60g)
- ○ 1/4 cup roasted red pepper, diced (30g)
- ○ 1/4 cup mushrooms, diced (30g)
- ○ 1/4 cup red onion, diced (30g)

Method

1. In a medium bowl, combine the whole wheat flour, active dry yeast, garlic powder, and salt.
2. Add the warm water and olive oil, and mix until all the ingredients are combined.
3. Knead the dough for 2-3 minutes, then cover the bowl with a kitchen towel and let it sit for 10 minutes.
4. Preheat the oven to 425°F (218°C).
5. On a lightly floured work surface, roll out the pizza dough.
6. Transfer the pizza dough to a baking sheet.
7. Spread the pesto on the pizza dough.
8. Top it with spinach, mozzarella cheese, roasted red pepper, mushrooms, and red onion.
9. Bake for 15 minutes.

Nutrition: 1 serving / whole meal, calories 301 / 1207, protein(g) 13 / 52, carbs(g) 28 / 112, fats(g) 15 / 62, fiber(g) 5 / 22, sodium(mg) 311 / 1244, sugar(g) 2 / 8, saturated fat(g) 3 / 13

Mushroom Veggie Pizza

8 servings

Prep: 20 min | Cook: 20 min | Total: 40 min

Ingredients

- ○ 1 lb pizza dough (follow the steps from the "Whole Wheat Veggie Pizza" (500g)
- ○ 2 tsp olive oil
- ○ 1/2 tsp garlic powder
- ○ 1 cup grated mozzarella (170g)
- ○ 1/2 cup grated feta cheese (125g)
- ○ 1/2 red onion, chopped (100g)
- ○ 1 red pepper, chopped (150g)
- ○ 1/2 cup mushrooms, sliced (75g)
- ○ 1/4 cup black olives, sliced (50g)
- ○ 2 tbsp dried oregano
- ○ 1/4 tsp salt

Method

1. Preheat the oven to 425°F (220°C).
2. Roll out the pizza dough. Place it on an oiled baking sheet.
3. Brush with olive oil and sprinkle with garlic powder.
4. Top with mozzarella and feta cheese.
5. Scatter red onion, red pepper, mushrooms, and black olives over the cheese.
6. Sprinkle it with oregano and salt.
7. Bake for 20 minutes, or until golden and crispy.
8. Enjoy!

Nutrition: 1 serving / whole meal, calories 408 / 3268, protein(g) 21 / 174, carbs(g) 27 / 222, fats(g) 24 / 197, fiber(g) 5 / 40, sodium(mg) 639 / 5113, sugar(g) 0 / 4, saturated fat(g) 14 / 116

Avocado & Pesto Pizza
8 servings

Prep: 15 min | Cook: 18 min | Total: 33 min

Method

1. Preheat the oven to 425°F (220°C).
2. Roll out the pizza dough. Place it on an oiled baking sheet.
3. Brush with olive oil and spread with pesto.
4. Sprinkle it with the cheese of your choice.
5. Top with avocado slices, cherry tomatoes, and pumpkin seeds.
6. Sprinkle it with garlic powder and salt.
7. Bake for 18 minutes, or until golden and crispy.
8. Enjoy!

Ingredients

- ○ 1 lb pizza dough (500g)
- ○ 2 tsp olive oil
- ○ 1/2 cup pesto (120g)
- ○ 1/2 cup Mozzarella cheese, grated (or feta, /parmessan) (85g)
- ○ 2 avocados, sliced
- ○ 1/2 cup cherry tomatoes, halved (85g)
- ○ 2 tbsp pumpkin seeds (20g)
- ○ 1/4 tsp garlic powder
- ○ 1/4 tsp salt

Nutrition: 1 serving / whole meal, calories 372 / 2981, protein(g) 8 / 71, carbs(g) 25 / 201, fats(g) 27 / 223, fiber(g) 8 / 66, sodium(mg) 125 / 1002, sugar(g) 1 / 8, saturated fat(g) 6 / 50

Tuna, Olives & Mushrooms Pizza
4 servings

Prep: 15 min | Cook: 20 min | Total: 35 min

Ingredients

- ○ 1 can of tuna (6oz / 170g)
- ○ 2 cups of mushrooms, any (200g)
- ○ 1 cup of black olives (140g)
- ○ 1 cup of marinara sauce (250ml)
- ○ 1 cup of mozzarella cheese (100g)
- ○ 1/2 cup of parmesan cheese (50g)
- ○ 1/4 cup of parsley, chopped (10g)
- ○ 1 large red onion
- ○ 1 large bell pepper
- ○ 1 large pizza crust (320g)
- ○ 2 tbsp olive oil
- ○ 1 tsp garlic powder
- ○ 1 tsp oregano
- ○ Salt and pepper

Method

1. Preheat the oven to 375 F/190C.
2. In a bowl, mix the tuna, mushrooms, olives, olive oil, garlic powder, oregano, salt, and pepper.
3. Spread the marinara sauce on the pizza crust.
4. Add the tuna, mushrooms, olives, and red onion on top.
5. Sprinkle mozzarella and parmesan cheese on top.
6. Bake for 20 minutes.
7. Garnish with parsley and bell pepper.
8. Enjoy!

Nutrition: 1 serving / whole meal, calories 640 / 2561, protein(g) 39 / 156, carbs(g) 38 / 152, fats(g) 34 / 139, fiber(g) 9 / 37, sodium(mg) 1418 / 5675, sugar(g) 3 / 13, saturated fat(g) 14 / 56

Measurement Conversions

CUP	ONCES	MILLILITERS	TBSP
1/16	1/2 oz	15 ml	1
1/8	1 oz	30 ml	3
1/4	2 oz	59 ml	4
1/3	2.5 oz	79 ml	5.5
3/8	3 oz	90 ml	6
1/2	4 oz	118 ml	8
2/3	5 oz	158 ml	11
3/4	6 oz	177 ml	12
1	8 oz	240 ml	16

ONCES	GRAMS
1/2 oz	14 g
1 oz	28 g
2 oz	57 g
5 oz	142 g
10 oz	284 g
15 oz	425 g
16 oz (1 pound)	455 g (≈ 500 g)
1.5 pounds	680 g
2 pounds	907 g (≈ 1 kg)

°F	°C
225°F	107°C
250°F	120°C
270°F	135°C
300°F	150°C
325°F	160°C
350°F	180°C
375°F	190°C
400°F	205°C (≈200°C)
425°F	220°C
450°F	235°C
475°F	245°C
500°F	260°C

Recipe Index

Made in United States
Orlando, FL
16 September 2024

51566578R00070